A personal
KIWI-YANKEE DIC

A personal
KIWI-YANKEE
DICTIONARY

Louis S. Leland Jr.

PELICAN PUBLISHING COMPANY
Gretna, 1984

First published in 1980 by John McIndoe Ltd.,
Dunedin, New Zealand

First Pelican printing, January 1984

Library of Congress Cataloging in Publication Data

Leland, Louis S.
  A personal Kiwi-Yankee dictionary.

  1. English language—New Zealand—Dictionaries.
2. English language—Provincialisms—New Zealand—
Dictionaries. 3. New Zealand—Dictionaries. I. Title.
PE3602.Z5L44   1984   427'.9931   83-22092
ISBN 0-88289-414-5

Cover drawing by Bruce B. Nye
Design by John McIndoe Ltd., Dunedin, New Zealand

Manufactured in the United States of America
Published by Pelican Publishing Company, Inc.
1101 Monroe Street, Gretna, Louisiana 70053

ACKNOWLEDGEMENTS

I have to thank every Kiwi who wittingly or unwittingly opened his or her mouth in my hearing. It is their words you will find here.

Foremost among these are my wife Freda who spoke, encouraged, proofread and advised on meanings, and Isabel Campbell, who typed the bulk of the dictionary, correcting spelling and advising on definitions as she worked (and who also asked, in Oliver's words, for 'more' work whenever the flow from my pen appeared to be slackening).

My panel of experts in the Kiwi tongue included Bazzer, against whose touchstone many of the questionable terms and definitions were tested, Annabel Cooper, Bruce Nye, Ian Hodgson, Raewyn Harray, and the whole Fliegner family who variously advised, proofread, filed, counted and most important of all, spoke in my presence. The Reference Department of the University of Otago Library also provided invaluable assistance with factual details.

As the years passed, it became more and more difficult for me to distinguish between New Zealand phrases and American ones. When this happened, I consulted with Roxane Smith and Dick Kammann, native experts in the esoteric tongues of Texas and Ohio.

FOREWORD

Designed to amuse as well as enlighten, this is a very personal dictionary. It is written in the first person to emphasize that it is a picture of New Zealand, its people and its language, through my eyes. As such it emphasizes one man's interests and reflects his attitudes.

Your picture of Kiwis and their land will of necessity differ. That's what makes horse races.

'Red sky at night, Shepherds' delight,
Red sky in the morning, Shepherds take warning.'

Not quite the way you learned it as a kid? That's New Zealand all over. 'Culture shock' in other countries comes from the radically different life-styles that you encounter. In New Zealand it is less obvious; it comes from things that look identical when you first see them, but are subtly or entirely different on closer inspection. Back in the days when I was attempting to learn French these were called faux amis (false friends), a list of these appears under F below.

This works both ways. My wife, a convent-schooled Kiwi bird (see below), went to California for a year of High School in her teens and on her first day in her first co-ed school, earned an entirely unfounded reputation by asking the boy sitting behind her if he had a rubber (see below). All she wanted was an eraser, but this experience colors her view of Americans to this day.

Not all Kiwis will recognize every entry in this collection, but most are in common use. Regional differences are indicated when known. To spare Kiwi readers culture shock note that all spellings, other than those of words in bold type, italics and/or enclosed in parentheses, conform to Yankee, not Kiwi, usage.

Note that use of the terms marked with a single asterisk (*) will mark your low social class, and those marked with two asterisks (**) are not for use in polite, or at least mixed, company.

Louis S. Leland, Jr.
Dunedin, 1979.

A & P Show: The Agricultural and Pastoral Society Show. Local equivalent of a STATE FAIR. This is a major event in every region and nearly all businesses, government departments, etc. close down for 'Show Day'. This is often a Friday and the first and most important day of the (usually) three-day show. Remember that New Zealand depends on sales of agricultural products (see: *primary products*) overseas for its living. Nearly everybody goes to the show (an urban couple I know well met at the pig exhibit 40 years ago). Sideshows, skill tests, horse jumping, rodeo exhibitions, polo matches, etc. etc. Don't miss it (if it has been raining wear your gumboots). (see: *gumboots*)!

a lamb is a sheep before you have carried it very far: Too true! Folk wisdom in New Zealand usually seems to go back to the farm. (see: *there must have been a stray bull in the paddock*)

abattoir: A SLAUGHTERHOUSE for meat for local consumption. Often owned and run by the larger cities, they do not have to meet the same health requirements as freezing works that slaughter for export. This seems to make no difference to the safety or taste of the food. (see: *freezer, freezing workers,* (the) *works*)

academic year (University): The academic year consists of 26 teaching WEEKS, starting at the end of February and going through the end of November. There are also three-week breaks in May and August. (see: *varsity, Uni, school, U.E., School Cert.)*

accelerator: When you wish to accelerate the speed of your automobile, you naturally press your right foot upon the accelerator (GAS PEDAL). (see: *bonnet, boot, handbrake, windscreen, mudguard*)

Acclimatization Society: A quasi governmental organisation divided into regions and run by elected representatives of those holding hunting and fishing licences. It is also financed by those licences although the central government does get a rakeoff. They stock the rivers with trout (and enforce the rules about catching them), count waterfowl and set bag limits, and support some game reserves. (see: *Plunket Society*)

act the goat: Someone who does a (see:) *down trou* is, in my opinion, PLAYING THE FOOL.

aerial topdressing: New Zealand's economic lifeline is her agricultural (particularly pastoral) produce. To deliver these products to North America, Europe and Japan at competitive prices, the inventive and industrious Kiwis have found ways to raise more and better food for less money. One key is the SPREADING of FERTILIZER FROM small single engine AIRCRAFT that take off from short grass strips (often comprising the total area of level land at the top of one ridge of an area of small ridges and valleys) and outperform most stunt fliers in their efforts to evenly cover the contracted area with powdered fertilizer (see: *Kiwi, primary products, super, manure).*

aerogramme: A flimsy blue sheet of paper on which airmail letters can be written and which folds up to make its own envelope. It is considerably cheaper to mail than is an airmail envelope with letter enclosed. Believe it or not, these are available in the U.S., where they are called AIR LETTERS. We try not to send these to North America to avoid the cheapskate impression. The rest of the world understands our parsimony.

age of consent: 16 YEARS (nuff said). Unless you want to marry her (or him) then you'll have to wait until she is 20 or get mum and dad to agree. (see: *mum, legal age for drinking*)

A.G.M.: Annual General Meeting. You will often hear people talking about the A.G.M. of a club or firm. This is the YEARLY BUSINESS MEETING of an organization. At this meeting, 'the committee' is elected. This group will run things with (usually) scant reference to the membership, for the other 364 days.

air conditioning: This is a tricky one since it is a 'true friend' if you are talking about cold, and a 'false friend' if you are talking about heat. 'Turn up the air conditioning' can and does mean, turn up the heat, rather more often than it refers to turning up the cooling system. Kiwis have logically concluded that alterations in both HEAT AND COLD amount to conditioning the air and that the one term should therefore refer to both. Very little of New Zealand has a climate in which air cooling is needed for any substantial proportion of the year which is why this dual purpose term more often refers to heating than cooling. (see: *central heating, false friends*)

air the washing: After drying wash on the line outside (local wisdom has it that clothes 'smell' and 'are' better after this treatment than they would be out of a drier. Some rude North American expatriates have suggested that this is making a virtue out of necessity), the clothing is put in a warm place, usually the cupboard where the hot water cylinder (tank) lives until it is toasty warm (aired). (see: *hot water cylinder, washhouse*)

All Blacks: Take the World Series winners, combine them with the Superbowl champs, add the prestige of a victorious Olympic team, and you have some faint idea of what this carefully chosen NATIONAL representative TEAM OF New Zealand's best RUGBY PLAYERS means to the nation. (Nearly) every boy wants to grow up to be one and most of the girls would just love to marry (or some reasonable facsimile thereof) one. If a Kiwi's (see: *Kiwi*) passions are, as commonly quoted, 'rugby, racing and beer', then the foremost of these is rugby and the All Blacks, its symbol. This may help you see why the Olympic boycott (1976) as a result of the All Black tour of South Africa affected many Kiwis just as an attack on the flag, motherhood, baseball and apple-pie would have affected Americans.

A quick illustration of their importance. On my arrival in New Zealand, I saved $10.00 by purchasing a white electric razor rather than an otherwise identical black one which was colored in honor of the All Blacks and accompanied by a picture of the team.

Note that these men are amateurs; there is almost no professional sport in New Zealand. (see: *football, Gleneagles Agreement*)

all flossied up: ALL TARTED UP. A nicer way of putting it.

alpine sticks or **frankfurters:** Available in the big city, these are tasty, OVERGROWN (extra long) HOT DOGS. Well worth sampling. (see: *bangers, saveloys and hot dogs*).

8

alsatian: A GERMAN SHEPHERD DOG. This breed has an unfortunate local reputation for viciousness. I suspect this is based on its use as police dogs and reinforced by selective attention to any incidents involving German shepherds. Dogs have a different social position in New Zealand than they do in North America. A dog is generally thought of as a working animal (used to herd sheep and cattle in a mainly pastoral country) and so not treated as a pet. Even urban Kiwis are often shocked at the idea that their pet dog might spend the night in the house. (see: *dogs, sausage dog, primary products*)

anti-clockwise: COUNTER-CLOCKWISE; the direction in which the ancient Druid inhabitants of Britain used to dance after painting themselves blue with woad. Remember: they were your cultural ancestors as well!

ANZAC biscuit: A COOKIE MADE OF rolled OATS and COCONUT. CARE packages sent to first world war N.Z. troops always included some of these. (see: *ANZAC DAY, biscuit*)

ANZAC day: On APRIL 25, 1915 a World War I campaign, strongly supported and partially planned by the then First Lord of the Admiralty (Winston Churchill) commenced. Combined Australian and New Zealand forces (ANZAC) hit one beach while French troops hit another. The French soon left but the ANZAC forces fought the Turks for 8½ long months before withdrawing in good order. A PUBLIC HOLIDAY is celebrated commemorating the heroism, loss of life (213,980 Commonwealth casualties) and waste of time and resources that the campaign entailed. Churchill resigned his government position and became an infantry battalion commander in France where, it has been suggested, he felt that at least any tactical errors made would be his own. (see: *ANZAC biscuits*)

ANZUS: The 'Security Treaty Between AUSTRALIA, NEW ZEALAND, AND THE UNITED STATES OF AMERICA', signed in 1951 committing each of these nations to '. . . act to meet the common danger in accordance with its constitutional processes . . .' (the New Zealand encyclopaedia says 'against the communist threat' but this wording isn't actually in the treaty). As far as I can tell, the treaty does not obligate any country to take any action (other than informing the United Nations Security Council) in the event of an armed attack upon one of the other signatories.

There has been some protest by a segment of the community against the visits of U.S. nuclear-powered navy vessels and the Prime Minister always cites the ANZUS treaty as justification for doing what he (and I, as if that mattered) wants to do anyway; namely welcome these visitors. This argument is based on Article II which says, in part, '. . . continuous and effective self help and mutual aid will maintain their individual and collective capacity to resist armed attack'.

Are you being served?: Can you imagine a salesgirl or salesman saying this? They do! A phrase out of another era when the social line between salesclerk and customer was much greater than today, when there could easily be an argument as to who has the higher social position. CAN I HELP YOU? (see: *salesclerk, clerk*)

Armed Offenders Squad: A S.W.A.T. TEAM. As the police are normally unarmed (as are criminals) this is a very special group of armed police called out to deal with armed criminals who have shown a willingness to use their weapons. Those occasions on which the Armed Offenders Squad is called out are sufficiently rare that such an event always makes the national (television and radio) news.

as silly as a two bob watch: Any timepiece that sells for 20c could be expected to keep somewhat irregular time, if any at all. Usually used to describe people, e.g. 'Jack is as silly as a two bob watch', implies eccentricity approaching the HAREBRAINED. (see: *bob*)

Associate Professor: A false friend (the term not the individual). While this is an academic rank and the same term is used as an academic rank in the U.S. they are not equivalent. Associate Professor N.Z. = PROFESSOR (but not department head) U.S. Another N.Z. term for the same academic rank is Reader. (see: *Professor, Chair, Lecturer, Reader, false friends*)

aubergine: An aubergine by any other name would be an EGGPLANT. (see: *veges, capsicum, swedes, courgette*)

Auckland (Central Auckland): Named for Lord Auckland, Viceroy of India in 1840, it comprises the area between Wellsford and Tuakau in the North Island including New Zealand's biggest metropolitan area, Auckland (742,786 people in the 1976 census). Nevertheless if sheep had the vote it would be all over. The Central Auckland region had 797,406 people in 1976 and 915,651 sheep. It is however, the only region in the country where the people outnumber the cattle (526,628). Good on you big smoke! (see: *good on you, big smoke, North Island*)

Aussie: (A) Someone from that slightly declassé suburb of New Zealand called Australia, an AUSTRALIAN;

(B) AUSTRALIA (see above). Despite northern hemisphere rumor to the contrary, Aussie and New Zealand are two very different (!) places. They are separated by a minimum of 1,200 miles of open water. Don't let anyone sell you shares in the Wellington-Sydney harbor bridge; at least if you purchase the connection between Brooklyn and Manhattan you can go look at 'your property'. Note that Kiwis tend to look down upon their Aussie brothers as being rather coarse, a condition deriving naturally from their purported descent from prisoners involuntarily exported from Britain to Botany Bay. On the other hand, Aussies tend to look down on New Zealand as a junior partner without the resources and get-up-and-go of Australia and Australians. (see: *Trans Tasman*)

award: an award, or more properly an Industrial Award is the CONTRACT BETWEEN UNION AND EMPLOYERS. Awards specify pay, fringe benefits, types of work etc.

B

bach: (say batch). A WEEKEND COTTAGE on lake, mountainside or coast. This term applies only to the 'North Island' (see: *crib, watch that, your thoughts are showing!*)

*backside: the politest term (it isn't very polite) for that portion of your anatomy on which you rest while in a SEATed position (see: *fanny, bum*)

backwards: Some aspect of each of the following is exactly opposite of what you would assume it to be: (see:)

bathwater	salt and pepper shakers
date	Saturday paper
dress circle	switches
driving	telephone dials
entree	walking
4 × 2	zippers

bad lot: A description of the other guy, or more likely, his son or daughter. 'He's a bad lot', is just a bit stronger than saying, 'he's NO GOOD.' This term usually applies to individuals rather than groups, and people rather than objects.

bags: 'I bags that red one'. I CLAIM that red one. Children's slang, probably originates from the hunter's practice of putting the game he shot into his game bag.

balaclava: A SKI MASK that covers all of the face and head except for the eyes. Just the thing for skiing down a glacier in winter (you don't need the balaclava in summer), or robbing a bank. Skiing down glaciers is an everyday occurrence in the South Island; bank robbery is unusual enough to make the national news, no matter where it happens.

ball frock: It's the 7th form ball (senior Prom) and she's dressed in her best BALL GOWN. Any formal dance is likely to be called a ball (and is likely to be one). Being under the influence is a much better excuse for violence or exhibitionistic behavior than it would be in North America. I have seen (at a black tie, formal dress, University graduation ball), a man peel off completely in the middle of the dance floor and climb a trellis to an overhanging balcony. (see: *down trou, school*)

ball of muscle: usually referring to children:

(A) a BALL OF FIRE (complimentary)

(B) a hyperactive child (derogatory)

Which of the two meanings is employed, depends more on the circumstances than the child.

Banda: Remember the duplicating machine that used to get the purple ink all over your fingers? A Banda is a DITTO machine. (see: *cyclostyle, drawing pins, Cellotape*)

bangers: New Zealand SAUSAGES. For those used to Oscar Meyer, they are best avoided. An inexpensive meal. This is a slang word, say 'sausages' in the butchery. (see: *saveloys, alpine sticks, butchery*)

barracks week: a WEEK OF voluntary R.O.T.C. for high schoolers.

bash: An informal PARTY. As 'she (that) was a good bash at your place last night. I've never been so pissed in my life'. (see: *she, pissed*)

*bastard: (A) It means what you think it does, but it can also be a term of ENDEARMENT and ADMIRATION. You are a right bastard, aren't you? (see: *hard shot, false friends*)

(B) A common variety of coarse metal FILE. (see: *long nosed pliers, false friends*)

Bastion Point: Shades of the occupation of Alcatraz by American Indians.

Bastion Point is a park in Auckland that was occupied by members of the Ngati Whaatua Maori group in much the same way and for much the same reasons. (see: *Waitangi Day, Maori*)

bathroom: literally means a ROOM CONTAINING a BATHTUB, a SINK, and nothing else. I have been embarrassed in the past to ask the way to the bathroom, and on arrival to find that the convenience I was looking for wasn't there. (see: *toilet, toilet paper, lav, loo, bog, grot, dunny*)

baths: The public baths are not places to get clean but SWIMMING POOLS, also called swimming baths. Before you say 'how quaint', remember what you call the clothing in which you swim. Now who's being illogical?

bathwater: There is a rumor that when you pull the plug the water runs out of your bath clockwise in the northern hemisphere and counter-clockwise down under. Well, if your bath is a symmetrical tank, preferably of some very stable substance like concrete, and it is firmly anchored, and the water in it has been there for a month or so (to get rid of random eddies introduced by pouring it in) and you devise a way to pull the plug straight down out of the bottom, then this is true. Otherwise, you pays your money and you gets either result in either hemisphere with about equal probability. (see: *backwards*)

Bazzer: An alternative pronunciation for the name BARRY. New Zealand is well populated with Bazzers and Trevs (Barrys and Trevors).

B.C.N.Z.: BROADCASTING CORPORATION OF NEW ZEALAND (formerly the N.Z.B.C.) a government owned but quasi independently controlled (e.g. T.V.A, U.S. Postal Services) body which operates both of N.Z.'s channels and about ¾ of its radio stations (see: *national programme, concert programme, wireless, N.Z.B.C., Zed*).

B.D.S.: Bachelor of Dental Surgery, your DENTIST who spends one year in ordinary university studies and five years in dental studies. Dentists, like physicians in New Zealand, do not have doctorates, and unlike physicians, do not even have the courtesy use of the title (see: *choppers, murder house, gum digger, M.B., Ch.B.*)

beaut: BEAUTIFUL in the sense of 'that was a beautiful dive into the swimming bath', or she's a beaut horse or sheila, etc. (see: *sheila*). Note that unfamiliar words in New Zealand are likely to be contractions of familiar ones, as beaut for beautiful, or speedo for speedometer, or park for parking place (see: *park*). Another distinct possibility is that they are familiar words pronounced in unfamiliar ways as revalley for reveille, or tomahto for tomato. (see: *vegs, strawbs, tomato/potato*)

be away — be away laughing: to SUCCEED EASILY. 'That driving test is in the hand, you'll be away laughing'. That driving test is easy, you'll pass with no sweat.

(The) Beehive: New Zealand has lots of conventional ones, and you must try manuka honey, but The Beehive isn't likely to produce anything so sweet. It is the latest and most controversial GOVERNMENT OFFICE BUILDING in Wellington, named for its shape.

(I've) been inside: I've been IN PRISON.

beer: If, as is commonly quoted, a Kiwi's passions are 'rugby, racing and beer' then beer is the most available and hence most commonly indulged passion. It is usually served in jugs, (pitchers that hold one liter these days, they used to hold 2 imperial pints or 1.2 U.S. quarts), sold in half g's (half imperial gallon bottles) and delivered to hotels (bars) in tank trucks. Shortly after my arrival in New Zealand, I commented to a friend on, what appeared to me to be, the vast amount of beer drunk by most of my acquaintances. (By the way, they couldn't believe the quantity of water I drank and were dumb-founded by the amount of ice I wanted in it.) He replied that it just wasn't true. Take himself for example; he only drank 3 jugs (3.6 U.S. quarts) when he went to the hotel and he rarely went to the hotel more than twice a week.

One other point. Kiwis don't like a foamy head on their beer and bartenders are skilled at pouring your beer without this head. Inquiry reveals that this is because they feel that the head is cheating (waste) and if you pay for 8 oz. of beer you should get 8 oz. A concern more with substance than froth. (see: *Kiwi, pissed, half g, jug, boozer, hotel, booze barn, sink a few, brew, six o'clock swill, skinful*)

beetroot: Red BEETS (just the thing for borscht) usually served in slices and found on every plate, in every salad and in every filled roll. Ugh! (see: *filled roll, marrow, swedes, silverbeet*)

beggared: (A) Probably derived from (see:) *buggered*, this is a polite way to indicate that you are TIRED OUT. 'I've been fencing with Sam all day and that bastard works so hard I'm beggared'. I've been stringing fences and putting in fenceposts with Sam all day, and that character works so hard I'm exhausted. (see: *buggered, bastard, stuffed, stonkered, bugger, buggering around*)

(B) DAMNED. 'I'll be beggared if I'll spend another day working with that sod.' (see: *sod*)

Belgium (sausage): LUNCHEON MEAT, sort of a low grade liverwurst. This is a South Island term only. It is interesting to note that this stuff was called German sausage prior to World War I. (see: *Friesian, Chinese gooseberry, false friends*)

belly-buster: is not an excess of candy and ice cream although the term conjures up interesting visions. It is the inexperienced swimmer's least favorite dive — a BELLY FLOP. (see: *honey pot/ bomb, duck dive*)

berk: a berk is a JERK. 'That berk then tried to change lanes right in front of me'. (see: *clot*)

Berkley: pronounced (Barkley) The name of a famous Irish Bishop (George Berkley, 1685-1753) who maintained that for each of us the world exists only as we perceive it through our senses. In the world inhabited by a color-blind man, there is no color.

An alternative view is that of Benjamin Wharf (an American engineer) who proposed that we think the thoughts and make the perceptual discriminations for which we have words. Therefore, a Kiwi sees the world differently from an American, because he analyses it through a somewhat different language (as you will have noted throughout this volume). A Frenchman or Russian would perceive a very different world indeed, according to this logic.

All this boils down to the observation that if you come from Berkley,

13

California, in New Zealand, you come from Barkley, California.

berko, or **to go berko:** GO BERSERK, committing violence upon persons and/or property. Kiwis go berko about as frequently and within the same class strictures as North Americans. The only difference is that if the person who goes berko is under the influence of alcohol, people arè likely to be much more understanding than in the U.S. or Canada. (see: *down trou*)

best of British luck, or **best of British:** Usually means, I WISH YOU GOOD LUCK BUT I DON'T THINK YOU HAVE A SNOWBALL'S CHANCE. For instance, when you ignore form at the races and bet on Lame Dog ('Ran well back in all previous races, never a chance') because he is paying $200-1, your mate, who bet on the favorite, is likely to wish you 'Best of British'. (see: *mate*)

*Bible basher: A very religious, often AGGRESSIVELY RELIGIOUS PERSON. This term is often applied to the door-to-door advocates of religion usually Fundamentalists or Mormon missionaries; however, anyone more religious than the speaker can earn this appellation.

bickies: BISCUITS meaning crackers or cookies. (see: *biscuit, water biscuit, big bickies*)

big bickies: LOTS OF MONEY. 'Sam just got promoted, he's in the big bickies now'. 'Sam just got promoted, he's in the high income bracket now'.

big smoke: 'Off to the big smoke are you?' Off to the BIG CITY are you? This phrase long predates concern about pollution and in fact is a term of approbation and admiration.

bike: usually a MOTORCYCLE not a bicycle. (see: *pushbike, motorbike, town bike, bikie*)

bikies: There are a number of MOTOR-CYCLE gangs in New Zealand whose young MEMBERS model themselves largely on the 'Hells Angels' although the all Maori 'Mongrel Mob' might not like that description. (see: *bike, motorbike*)

bilberry: Bilberry ice cream, bilberry cheesecake, sorry no go, English bilberry (BLUEBERRY) jam is the best you can do in New Zealand, although hopeful rumors of experiments in growing these in New Zealand have reached my wagging ears. (see: *strawberries*)

billion: If you could find a Kiwi billionaire (which you can't) he would be much richer than his U.S. counterpart, since a billion in New Zealand is equal to a TRILLION in the U.S. That is to say:

1 billion U.S. = 1,000,000,000

1 billion N.Z. = 1,000,000,000,000 (see: *thousand million*)

bird: There are two major types of birds. There is the feathered kind that you are familiar with, and the (to my mind) much more attractive featherless kind. I suppose that gentlemen hippopotami feel the same way about lady hippos. A bird is a GIRL. A 'bit of bird' is therefore . . . (see: *sheila, bit of crumpet, bit of fluff*)

Biro: A brandname that has become a noun. Biros are BALLPOINT PENS. You very likely won't be understood if you refer to a ballpoint, the word is biro. (see: *Snowtex, Witches-Britches*)

biscuit: Any sort of COOKIE or CRACKER is a biscuit. What you think is a biscuit is a scone. (see: *scone, cookie, bickies, water biscuits*)

bit of all right: 'She's a bit of all right'. VERY ATTRACTIVE.

*bit of crumpet: (A) a SEXY LASS. (see: *bit of fluff, crumpet, bird*)

(B) COITUS (see: *shag, have it off, get one away, root, on with, stuff,* (a) *naughty*)

bit of fluff: A patronising description of a young lady. The term tends to reflect more on the intentions and attitudes of the speaker than the attributes of the subject. A FEATHER-BRAINED GIRL.

It has been suggested that the fluff in question is made up of the lady's natural feathery covering usually hidden by the bottom of her bikini. (see: *bird, bit of crumpet*)

bit on the side: MISTRESS.

bitumen: What your driveway is probably surfaced with — ASPHALT.

blimin': As in 'some blimin' thing'. Actually it's the local version of 'blooming' and means 'darned'. (see: *bloody, flaming, ruddy*)

bloke: A MAN. 'He's a good bloke'.

**bloody: Often used in referring to the British (bloody Pommies), Inland Revenue (tax collectors) etc. For most people, it occupies approximately the same place in the Kiwi lexicon as 'DAMN' does in ours. (Damn Yankees anyone?) However, for some it is an extremely strong and highly objectionable word. I have heard it suggested that this comes from a double entendre 'By our Lady' stated as an insult to the Catholic Mary Queen of Scots, implying that she and the Virgin had little in common. It also suggested that she was physiologically female. (see: *blimin, winge, flaming, bloody minded*)

bloody minded: From the point of view of the individual to whom you are applying this appellation he is probably sticking to the letter of the law. From your point of view he is being DIFFICULT, OBSTRUCTIONISTIC, RIGID and OBNOXIOUS. (see: *bloody*)

blow it: (A) A relatively polite way of saying 'to hell with it', or 'I GIVE UP'.

(B) 'I'm afraid I will blow it'. 'I'm afraid I will FAIL.' (see: *done your chips*)

bludger: a bludger is a SPONGER — someone who is always borrowing and rarely repaying. To bludge is to borrow. It's socially acceptable to say 'may I bludge a cigarette (or a cup of sugar)' but calling someone a bludger can be a fighting insult. (see: *cadge*)

blue: a GOOF or mistake. 'I made a blue in trying to get on with her on the first date'. (see: *boob, on with*)

Blue Duck: A strange New Zealand bird (feathered). Unlike most other ducks in the world, this one lives in swift flowing mountain streams. It looks as if it has a moustache, since the beak has two flaps at the end that are used to strain caddis fly larvae out of the streams for dinner. The Maori name is WHIO because that's what its call sounds like. (see: *bird*)

bob: Now it means a *dime*. It used to mean 12 pence but decimalization changed everything to 10's. Yes, New Zealand used to have (pre-10 July, 1967) the same incomprehensible monetary system as the Mother country. (see: *quid, not the full quid, as silly as a two-bob watch, decimalization, metrication, pound, shilling, sixpence, penny*)

Bobby: Often used for the COP on the beat. Part of New Zealand's British heritage.

bod: a PERSON. Derived from body as 'I need a few bods for this job'. It is perfectly ordinary parlance and not in the least derogatory. (see: *odd bod*)

*bog (a): a SOJOURN on the TOILET.

*bog (the): TOILET. (Not a term used by the most refined.) Also refers to an area of swampy ground, but you knew that already. (see: *toilet, toilet paper, lav, loo, grot, dunny*)

*bog in: BEGIN to engage enthusiastically in an ACTIVITY usually eating. (see: *Kiwi grace, bog*)

bollicking; When you rush into the house to give your wife a big kiss and she screams at you for tracking mud across her nice clean carpet, the CHEWING-OUT you are getting is a bollicking. Whether it's a rocket from your boss or a dressing-down by your nearest and dearest, a bollicking is no fun.

**bong: A term borrowed from Australia where it is used to refer to aborigines; in New Zealand, it is a derogatory reference to Maoris and occasionally Pacific Islanders. This is a fighting word; use it only if your neck is red and you enjoy a punch up. (see: *coconut, Maori, punch-up, wog*)

bonkers: NUTS. Someone who is bonkers has a screw loose. (see: *drive you crackers*)

bonnet: that's the HOOD of your car and you had better remember that, because hood won't be understood. (see: *boot, windscreen, accelerator, handbrake, mudguard*)

Bonus Bonds: The New Zealand Post Office, in addition to operating an efficient mail service, also runs the telephone system and operates a bank (with tellers in every Post Office). This bank issues (among many other things) Bonus Bonds which bear no interest but which participate in a monthly lottery (every dollar is one chance) until cashed in. The prizes, like all gambling winnings by non-professionals, are not subject to income tax. A local organization has calculated that the overall return on these is about 2%, but we can all dream. (see: *Golden Kiwi, Post Office*)

boob: a GOOF or boo-boo. e.g. 'I made a boob.' It can also mean what you think it does.

booeye: So far OUT IN THE COUNTRY, mountains, or woods that carrier pigeons lose their way trying to find the nearest town. (see: *wops or wop-wops*)

(to) book: To MAKE A RESERVATION at a place of entertainment where one 'books a seat' or at an eating establishment where one 'books a table'.

boomer: 'She's a boomer.' REALLY GOOD. (see: *mighty*).

boot: Can be used for the things you hike in, and there is an expression 'to put the boot in' which means metaphorically to kick someone, as 'then he really put the boot in and sent him down the road' (fired him); or gave him the boot. However, the commonest use of boot refers to what you would call the TRUNK of your car. (see: *bonnet, windscreen, accelerator, handbrake, mudguard*)

booze barn: Any large open room devoted to the 'purveyance of spirituous liquors'. One of these, that I used to frequent, in a provincial center measures approximately 50 ft by 300 ft of open room with a bar that spans ¾ of the 300 ft wall. There has been some argument that the neighbourhood pub should return and replace such barns. To a limited extent, this has actually been happening, in that new pub construction tends to be smaller and cozier. (see: *hotel, boozer, tavern, beer, six o'clock swill*).

boozer: the place where you drink. 'Meet you down at the boozer (BAR)'. Except for a few new-fangled 'taverns' the boozer is always, by legal requirement, part of a place that (at least nominally) offers bed and board as well, and is consequently called a hotel. (see: *hotel, beer, bottle store, booze barn, six o'clock swill, licensed hotel, plonk*)

borer: Wooden antiques and houses must be carefully inspected for the presence of myriad tiny holes looking like randomly scattered periods produced by a mad typist. These are made by a local insect with the dendrophagic habits of a TERMITE. If there are many of these holes, it is said that the object is held together by all the borer holding hands. In the earlier stages, this condition is curable by fumigation or, if holes are few, using a syringe to shoot kerosene into each hole.

Boston buns: This term refers to a sweet bun, filled with jam or cream and iced with coconut. (see: *bread roll, iced buns*)

bottle store: Attached to every licensed hotel is not only a boozer, but a separate shop which sells your home supplies of booze. In other words, a LIQUOR STORE or PACKAGE STORE. (see: *hotel, licensed hotel*)

bottom drawer: The place where young ladies (and perhaps some of their male counterparts) store away those things which will enable them to set up housekeeping when grown and married. If you can't afford a HOPE CHEST you always have a bottom drawer. (see: *glory box*)

bowler: (A) the PITCHER in a cricket game. (see: *bowling*)

    (B) Someone who plays bowls (there are two ten pin alleys, that I know of, in N.Z. but that isn't bowling, that's 10 pin) (see: *bŏwling*)

    (C) A bun shaped HAT. Not often seen these days.

bowling: (A) indoor and outdoor, and neither of these is 10-pin bowling. This refers to the game of bowls which is a cross between shuffleboard (without sticks and with six-inch diameter balls substituted for the pucks) and horseshoe pitching. This is usually done on lawns like putting greens (only flatter) by white clad (obligatory!) middle aged (optional) sportsmen and women (separately, of course).

    (B) pitching the ball in a cricket game (see: *bowler*)

bowsers: No, this has nothing to do with beer. A bowser is a GAS (petrol) PUMP. 'Pull up to the bowsers and I'll fill her up'. (see: *petrol*)

box of birds: 'How are you today?' 'I'm a box of birds today'. (I'm on top of the world, RIGHT AS RAIN.)

box of fluffy ducks: I'm a box of fluffy ducks? I'm just as WELL/HAPPY/SUCCESSFUL AS CAN BE. (see: *box of birds*)

boxer shorts: Sorry, if you wear these you will have to go to Aussie (Australia) to get them or have them sent from home. No-one here wears them and most sales clerks wouldn't even known what you were talking about if you asked for them. (see: *sales clerks*)

Boxing Day: A pugilists' bacchanalia. Well, no, but I couldn't resist. Traditionally, on the DAY AFTER CHRISTMAS, wealthy Englishmen and their ladies used to have their servants box up the leftovers from Christmas dinner and distribute this largesse (sometimes along with a few presents) to the local poor. The custom has died but the name hasn't. (see: *Christmas*)

boys on the hill: Not usually the boys in the band. This phrase refers to the MEMBERS OF PARLIAMENT, New Zealand's unicameral legislature. (see: *Parliament*)

braces: Remember those elasticized straps over your shoulders that held up your pants in the dim and distant? Well, if you want a pair of SUSPENDERS, just ask for braces. (see: *suspenders*)

brandy snaps: A latticework cigar-shaped CONFECTION made of golden syrup, flour, ginger, brandy essence, etc. stuffed with cream and calories. (see: *golden syrup*)

brass me off: TO MAKE ME ANGRY.

brassed off: ANGRY.

bread: It comes in standard-sized loaves (government regulation). 350g ($\simeq$12 oz), 500g ($\simeq$1 lb), 700g ($\simeq$1½ lb). Unfortunately, common parlance for these loaves differs between the North and South islands.

Many of the 700g loaves are made like a camel with two humps so that they can conveniently be split in half. Usually, if you ask for a loaf in the South Island it is one of these two humps (350g) that you get. In the North Island, if you want the same amount of bread (350g) you must ask for a half loaf.

The other thing about bread, is that in this land of abundant food, where restaurant servings are usually generous, it is very hard to get more than one piece of bread (or one roll). Unlike North America, where they seem to hope you will settle for smaller servings if you fill up with bread, in New Zealand restaurants appear afraid that you will spoil your appetite with the stuff. (see: *North Island, South Island, mainland, pig island, quarter white*)

bread rolls or **hamburger rolls:** These come in two basic shapes — hamburger buns and HOT DOG BUNS. The terms, hamburger roll or bread roll, are used for both shapes. The term bread roll usually refers to hot dog buns. No-one has ever heard of a hot-dog bun; few have heard of what you would call a hot dog for that matter, although there is a thing on a stick that goes by that name. (see: *bangers, saveloys, alpine sticks, hot dogs, sandwich, hamburger*)

break wind: To release internally generated gases through one's anal orifice. A genteel expression.

(a) brew: a GLASS OF BEER. (see: *beer*)

(the) British disease: STRIKES. (see: *industrial unrest, industrial action*)

brolly: That's what you hold over your head to keep the rain off (an UMBRELLA).

brown derby: A CONE, usually OF plain (vanilla) ICE CREAM, with the ice cream part DIPPED IN hot CHOCOLATE which quickly hardens around it.

Very tasty. This term is used only in the South Island. It is a chocolate dip in the North Island.

bubble: A fishing FLOAT. Most often made of clear plastic with a plug on one side so that you can weight it with water. (see: *trace wire, false friends*)

bubble and squeak: If someone offers you 'bubble and squeak' it isn't the latest breakfast cereal, it's VEGETABLE HASH. Chop up yesterday's left-over veges and fry them up with a bit of butter. (see: *veges*)

bubbly: Any SPARKLING WINE but most particularly champagne. 'The ladies always like a drop of the bubbly'. (see: *champers*)

buck in: The Mayor of Greymouth was on TV recently, praising the townsfolk for the way they bucked in (PITCHED IN) to help the city and each other during a flood. (see: *muck in*)

bucket of bolts: a JALOPY.

**bugger: A term of derision. When used as a noun, it refers to someone you don't like. When used as a verb, it refers to the male act of SODOMY with a member of one's own sex and species. (see: *buggering around, buggered, beggared, sod*)

*buggered: EXHAUSTED, worn out, beat. Obviously deriving from the putative state of someone who has been sodomized, it has lost all but the faintest hint of this origin. There are other ways to declare your imminent collapse. (see: *beggared, stonkered, stuffed, bugger, buggering around*)·

bugger off: GO AWAY.

*buggering around: 'He's been buggering around with that job for weeks'. WASTING TIME. (see: *bugger*)

*bum: is what you sit on. Les femmes in New Zealand appear to have an unusually high proportion of broad ones and sturdy legs to match. Pioneer heritage? (see: *backside, fanny*)

bummer: A BAD TRIP, drug or just everyday activity, as, 'yesterday was a bummer'.

bun: as in 'use your bun' (HEAD). (see: *scone*)

bun in the oven: PREGNANT. (see: *up the spout, up the duff, sprog*)

bunch of fives: Hold out your hand flat, palm up. Now curl the index finger into the palm, now the middle finger, now the ring finger, now the little finger. Put your thumb across the backs of the middle sections of the index and middle fingers. Now shake this FIST under someone's nose and ask, in a belligerent tone of voice if he'd like a 'bunch of fives'. (see: *knuckle sandwich*)

Bursary: 7th formers (or bright sixth formers in the 'right' schools) (17-18 years old) take this exam to earn some financial support (above tuition, for University). The top 4% of Bursary passers who do some extra exams (Schols — scholarship) get a little more. These amounts are not large but they are the icing on the cake. Each N.Z. student under 21 who is accepted by a University gets the 'standard tertiary bursary' of about $23 per week. If he has completed 7th form successfully and has been awarded a 'Higher School Certificate' he gets his tuition paid. On top of this a Bursary exam pass of higher than 250 out of 500 gives him an extra $100 per year. 300-500 gives him $150 per year, and a Schols pass gives him $300 per year. These latter amounts are net, not additive. (see: *nett,* *school, School Cert., U.E.*)

bush: FOREST or JUNGLE (see: *bushwacker*)

bush carpenter: Those of us who are more concerned with function than looks. You know, the nail may be in crooked, but it holds.

bushwacker: not an evil man in a black stetson who shoots people in the back from ambush, but simply a MAN WHO WORKS in the backwoods or BUSH. (see: *hard case, false friends*)

butchery: This is not your local slaughterhouse (see: *works or meatworks, abattoir*), but rather an institution you may be old enough to remember. The neighborhood BUTCHER'S SHOP. 'And not too much fat on that, Mr John'. (see: *T bone, fillet, topside, silverside*)

by crikey: BY GOLLY (gosh). (see: *by ginger*)

by ginger: BY GOSH (golly). (see: *by crikey*)

B.Y.O.B.: on a party invitation, means BRING YOUR OWN BOTTLE.

C

cadge: (cad-je) — TO BORROW. 'May I cadge a cup of sugar?' 'Sam is a perennial cadger. I wouldn't lend him anything if I were you.' (see: *bludger*)

*(your) cake hole: is your MOUTH. Neither friendly nor commonly used, avoid this one. 'Shut your cake hole'.

Califont: You may rent a flat that has a SMALL GAS WATERHEATER over the tub or shower. You switch this on and it roars into life, startling the hell out of you and providing the frightening sight and sound of a violent conflagration that quickly heats the water. (see: *hot water cylinder*)

call: I recently received an official message from an organ of the N.Z. Government asking me to '. . . call if convenient, otherwise telephone.' To call means to COME IN PERSON, it does not mean 'to telephone'. (see: *Post Office*)

can off: 'Then he went round the corner and canned off his bike which went on to win the race without him'. Then he went round the corner and fell (violently) off his motorcycle which . . . FALL (VIOLENTLY) OFF (see: *bike, come a greaser, come a gutser, can out*)

can out: to OVERTURN one's yacht, canoe, or other WATERBORNE CRAFT under circumstances that imply that this was not your intention. (see: *yachtie, can off*)

candy floss: That light, airy, sweet, carnival fare COTTON CANDY. It seems a much more elegant name. (see: *toffee apple*)

cane: A verb referring to the practice of applying a supple switch vigorously to the backside of an errant schoolboy (it is illegal to cane girls, clearly a case where it is only just that equality for the ladies should be energetically pursued). Most any adult male Kiwi will be happy to recall his caning(s) (PADDLINGS) during his schooldays. Private schools seem to distribute these more freely than public ones and a sociologist (American) claims that there is a bonding process between Masters and boys brought about by the caning process. Every boy appears to feel that

20

to be caned once is a necessary proof of manhood. Some boys, however, appear to collect canings, keeping a tally of beatings on their belts. Everyone has to be special in some way. (see: *get the strap, backside*)

canoe: The usual meaning of canoe in New Zealand is an eskimo KAYAK, just the thing for shooting the rapids of New Zealand's many tumultuous mountain streams. What you think of as a canoe, is a Canadian canoe or an Indian canoe to a Kiwi, and he's probably never seen one.

Canterbury: comprises the middle ⅔rds of the east coast of the South Island extending westwards into the Alps. The wide flat and fertile Canterbury Plains is some of the best farming land in N.Z.

Canterbury also includes N.Z.'s most English city, Christchurch (metropolitan area population 295,296, 1976), with stone buildings and a very English cathedral. Take a trip up to 'The Sign of the Takahe' in the Port Hills above Christchurch for a Devonshire tea. The building is fascinating, the view spectacular and the tea fattening. Here (Canterbury) too is Mt. Cook, N.Z.'s highest mountain set in a national park of wilderness, glaciers, and mountains (a must). Canterbury's (1976 census) statistics are as follows: 428,586 people, 10,751,000 sheep and 570,000 cattle. (see: *South Island, tea*)

capping: In May of each year, the seven University level institutions hold their GRADUATIONS after a week of traditional hi-jinks. These include parades, skirted (not kilted) male bag-pipe players entering every bar in town to give off-key concerts and multiple large scale practical jokes. The police tend to look tolerantly at such activities during this week. Why, you may ask, is graduation in May when the academic year runs from March through November? Well, when all final exam papers had to go by ship to Great Britain to be graded, the results just didn't come back until the following May. The exams no longer go to the Mother Country, but the time of graduation hasn't changed. (see: *capping concert, capping mag, procession*)

capping concert: At graduation time each year, the students of a number of New Zealand's Universities put on a musical stage show. Sometimes they are risque, sometimes downright crude, but always funny. One warning, if you sit in the front few rows you may find yourself an involuntary participant in the activities on stage. (see: *capping, capping mag*)

capping mag: or capping magazine is the GRADUATION week STUDENT PUBLICATION. It serves one official purpose, to provide a list of all the graduates, and a host of unofficial ones. It is the students' chance to satirize their elders and their society, morals, politics, education, all fair game. Capping magazines range between witty and obscene. Many cities have restricted the sale of these magazines in time or place but none have quite dared to ban them outright.

capsicum: An elegant name for a GREEN PEPPER. (see: *veges, aubergine, swedes, courgette*)

caramel: pronounced KARMEL as in Carmel, California. Still good candy. (see: *Berkley*)

caravan: In far off days of yore, these crossed the deserts, strings of camels

21

swaying, chewing and spitting in the breeze. Today I'm afraid it is a remote and prosaic, but comfortable, descendant of that romantic, but smelly and uncomfortable, parade. In short, a HOUSE TRAILER. Note that most of these are small and mobile, partly as a result of a law which forbids their use as a permanent residence. Hence all motorcamps have strictly temporary accommodation. (see: *motorcamps*).

carbonettes (North Island): hard packed BRIQUETS of COKE. Long and hot burning. The biggest bit of culture shock I've experienced in New Zealand was moving from the North Island, where these are sold in every neighborhood store (dairy) and gas (petrol) station, to the South Island and trying to buy some. No one knew what I was talking about. (see: *dairy, petrol, mainland*)

cardigan or **cardie:** A SWEATER that is cut like a jacket in that it buttons up the front. These grow more common as you go south into the colder weather. Sweater sets that include cardigans are popular with some of the ladies. (see: *twin set and pearls, jumper*)

careering: 'And then the lorry, whose brakes had failed, came careering down the hill'. And then the truck, whose brakes had failed, came CAREENING down the hill.

cark out: to GO TO SLEEP, often as a result of alcohol intake or exhaustion, or to DIE.

carless days: On the 30th July 1979, New Zealand introduced a drastic fuel conservation measure (in addition to banning petrol sales on week-ends). This was the banning of the operation of all privately and petrol powered motor vehicles weighing 4,400 lbs or less (except for motor-cycles) for one day per week. That day to be chosen by the owner of the vehicle in question. There are several exceptions, public transport (taxis, buses, ambulances) rental cars and those (about 20% of vehicles) who have a good reason to drive on their carless day. You will see a green sticker with a white X upon it next to the red carless day sticker on the windscreens of the exempt vehicles.

The introduction of this measure created some unexpected difficulties, e.g. the most popular days turned out to be Wednesday and Thursday, while the government had expected (and printed stickers for) the weekend.

As far as effects go, research has shown that it certainly has alleviated the parking problem on Wednesday and Thursday. As far as saving petrol goes, the absolute savings over the previous year brought about by both savings measures combined is $\simeq 2.8\%$. The notional savings, assuming that demand would have grown if steps hadn't been taken, is $\simeq 8.5\%$. You pays your money and takes your choice. (see: *petrol*)

carnie kid: JAIL BAIT (see: *age of consent*).

car park: is a place in which automobiles can find temporary surcease from their labors in the salubrious open air. A PARKING LOT.

cassia: If you have an American cookbook, and it calls for CINNAMON, use what is called cassia in New Zealand otherwise you will wonder why it doesn't taste quite right (with thanks to Mrs Bear). (see: *cinnamon*)

casual meals: If you go to a hotel restaurant for a meal or telephone for a booking (reservation), you will be asked if you are '. . . in the house or casual'. Unless you are a registered guest, your answer should be 'casual'. (see: *hotel*)

cat: the New Zealand branch of the felis domesticus family makes its North American cousins (on average) look like kittens. An average adult cat weighs upwards of a stone (14 pounds). (see: *stone, pussy*)

cattle stop: In a pastoral country with 60,000,000 sheep and 3,000,000 people, opening and closing gates can get to be a terrible nuisance. The cattle stop is a horizontal arrangement of railway rails with 4-inch gaps between them set into the road at a break in the fence. The cattle and sheep jam their hooves between the rails and find it easier to stay on their own side. (see: *Taranaki Gate*)

caucus: When I first came to N.Z. I assumed that the laws of the country were made in Parliament. However, after listening to Parliament on the radio for a few years it became clear that the debates were totally irrelevant and that those Bills sponsored by the government (majority party) always passed, everyone else's were always defeated and no one ever seemed to cross party lines on any vote (it does happen but so rarely as to be totally negligible). So who makes the decisions? My next hypothesis was that it was really a dictatorship with the Prime Minister calling all the shots (this is not an unpopular theory in 1979) (see: *Muldoon*). It turns out that there is meaningful debate on the government sponsored Bills but this debate takes place in private. Each party holds caucus meetings consisting of all the representatives of that party in Parliament. Debate is presumably free and fierce in these caucus meetings and this is the place WHERE DECISIONS ARE actually MADE! Once a decision is made, party discipline is strong and all members of the party caucus are expected to support the group decision independent of their own judgement. Presumably if someone didn't he would lose his voice in caucus and his seat at the next election. (see: *Parliament, boys on the hill, National Party, Labour Party, shadow cabinet ministers, M.P.*)

caught short: an immediate need to see a man about a dog. An explanation to any shopkeeper that you've been caught short will usually result in an immediate offer of his toilet facilities, or directions to nearby public ones. Strangely enough, it is only men who seem to use this phrase. Either the ladies are better planners, have better control, or just know something we don't.

Cellotape: SCOTCH TAPE (see: *cyclostyle, drawing pins*)

cement block: a CINDERBLOCK. I think the Kiwis have the right of this one.

central heating: Not bloody likely mate (except for a few effete sorts, probably North American or Pommie (which see) immigrants). 'Do you know why you Yanks get so many colds? It's because you keep your houses so hot the contrast gives you colds'. It is customary, even in the coldest parts of the country (the U.S. Antarctic support team is based in Christchurch), to turn the heat off completely at night, and most people consider 65°F a warm house. (see: *air conditioning*)

(the) chain: In the freezing works where meat animals are butchered for New Zealand's most lucrative export trade, there is a kind of disassembly line where each person chops out the same portion of each carcass as it reaches him on an endless belt. Extremely boring, but by local standards, extremely well paid work and considered the choice job to have in the works. (see: *works, freezing works*)

Chair: (A) What you sit in.

(B) The ACADEMIC ESTABLISHMENT held by a University Professor, e.g. The Chair of Physics at Auckland University. (see: *Professor, false friends*)

champers: weddings, wedding breakfasts, celebrations of all kinds call for CHAMPAGNE. (see: *bubbly*)

charge hand: The Japanese would call him the honcho, you would tend to say FOREMAN. This latter term (foreman) is also used in New Zealand. (see: *leading hand*)

Charlie Browns: Lace up BROWN SHOES with crepe soles FOR KIDS. Remember *Buster Brown* shoes?

*charlies: A slang term for the physical characteristics which identify the female homo sapien as a mammal.

chat up: is to engage in conversation. Usually this refers to a discussion with a member of the opposite sex whom one has met for the first time. 'I saw you chatting up that beaut sheila at the hotel last night'. I saw you TALKING IN AN ANIMATED AND ENGAGING WAY with that beautiful girl in the bar last night. (see: *beaut, sheila, hotel*)

cheek: The guy who invites himself to dinner and then complains about the quality of the food has this in excess. GALL or HUTZPA. (see: *false friends*)

cheeks: A term most commonly used to refer to one's BUTTOCKS, although it is also used for the fleshy parts of the face. (see: *false friends*)

cheerios: These round little 'O' 's bursting with . . . Sorry, wrong again. *Kellogs* has floated to these distant shores but wisely they have avoided confusion by not introducing this item. In New Zealand Cheerios are COCKTAIL FRANKFURTERS. The rude and lewd also call these 'little boys'. (see: *bangers, saveloys, alpine sticks, false friends*)

cheery bye: a cheerful GOODBYE. (see: *hurray*)

cheesed off: When my tax bill arrives, I am usually very cheesed off (a cross between ANGRY and ANNOYED). (see: *Inland Revenue*)

chemist shop: The place where you purchase your chemicals such as acetylsalicylic acid, vitamin B_1, shampoo etc. In other words, a DRUG STORE. These establishments come much closer to being genuine drug stores than their North American counterparts, since they sell little beyond drugs, cosmetics and toilet articles.

chilly bin: A literal description of the inside of the ideal PICNIC HAMPER, made of foamed polystyrene. You put in frozen *Slikka* pads and you've got a well-insulated portable refrigerator. If you tour New Zealand by car (or bicycle) one of these will save you money and let you lunch in the most beautiful spots. (see: *Slikka pads, coolibah*)

chin wag: a CHAT or a good old fashioned gossip.

Chinese gooseberries: Brown and hairy on the outside, bright green on the inside and about the size and shape of an egg. You may know this as KIWI FRUIT, since the New Zealand merchants changed the name in order to facilitate sales to the United States during the days when the U.S. didn't officially recognize Red China's existence.

After a night chilling in the 'fridge, (don't say ice-box, New Zealand went from counting on the coolith of the evening to refrigerators with no intervening steps, so no one knows what an ice-box is) the Chinese gooseberry makes my favorite breakfast. I just slice off the widest end and scoop out the rest with a teaspoon. Highly recommended. (see: *goosegog, tamarilloes*)

chip: A North Island term for a SMALL BOX of berries, the equivalent of (see:) *punnet*, also a North Island term. The South Island term (Christchurch south), is (see:) *pottle*.

chippies: (A) Those crunchy thin slices of fried potato (POTATO CHIPS).
One of my first language laughs in New Zealand was a sign in the Palmerston North Opera House which said:

NO CHIPPIES
ALLOWED

I hadn't realized that soliciting was such a serious problem although every city has its (legal) solicitors. (see: *solicitors, false friends, Opera House*)

(B) The men who produce chips and sawdust as a regular part of their work (CARPENTERS).

chippolatas: frankfurter shaped spicy sausages, not recommended. (see: *bangers, saveloys*)

chips: These are FRENCH FRIES. Don't let the fact that some take-away bars advertise french fried potatoes fool you. If you were to ask for them you'd most likely get a blank look. You must ask for chips. (see: *fish and chips, take-aways*)

chocka: Fibber McGee's closet could have been accurately described as chocka. For younger readers, it will have to be Scrooge McDuck's money bin. Chocka means FULL to bursting.

chocolate wheel: At school fairs and other charity gatherings, the chocolate wheel is a traditional fundraiser. This is a WHEEL OF FORTUNE with a box of chocolates for the person who has purchased the ticket marked with the winning number. Occasionally other prizes are offered (e.g. chickens) but chocolates are the staple.

chook: Another name for one of the most expensive meats in New Zealand. If a Kiwi invites you to dinner, odds are about 4 to 1 that he (she really) will serve CHICKEN. This is because it isn't long since chicken was the very most expensive meat in New Zealand and in many households was served only for Christmas and honored guests. Even the advent of Colonel Sanders hasn't eliminated this heritage.

choppers: (A) 'Sink your choppers into that chook and you'll think you died and went to heaven'. TEETH decay faster in New Zealand than they do in Britain according to a recent investigating commission (soil deficiencies?). Dental bills, however, are laughably low in New Zealand by North American standards. Would you believe $75.00 for a root canal job or $11.00 for an ordinary amalgam filling? (see: *B.D.S., chook*)

*(B) Slang term for Malaysians, used on some University campuses.

(see: *bunga, wog, coconut*)

Christmas: That lovely time of year when all the shops shut up (and many of them remain closed through January as well), the sun shines and the beach beckons. Most people do eat a traditional (cold weather) English Christmas dinner, and exchange gifts, but otherwise there is no resemblance. This is the start of the summer holidays when the cities empty and the resorts fill. Bloody marvelous, unless you want to get some work done. If your work involves anyone else, just forget it! (see: *New Zealand Christmas Tree, January, school holidays, Father Christmas, cracker, Boxing Day*)

Christmas cracker: (see: *cracker*)

Christmas drinks: It is a time-honored tradition that you have your friends over before Christmas and ply them with liquor and little goodies. In fact, this is the (see:) *bottle store's* best time of year and a common enquiry is 'have you bought your Christmas booze yet?' (see: *New Zealand Christmas tree, Christmas*)

chuffed: a combination of cheered up and puffed up. When I see my name in print (over an article) I am PROUD AND HAPPY (chuffed).

chunder: a term which is used freely by people who engage in occasional massive over-indulgence in alcoholic beverages; regurgitate. (see: *technicolour yawn*)

ciggies: cigarettes (see: *veges*)

cinnamon: A somewhat milder taste than you would expect. Do not use this in American recipes when they call for cinnamon. Use cassia instead. (see: *cassia*)

city: A collection of human habitations is by law entitled to call itself a CITY when it has achieved the overwhelming population attributed to a name OF such dignity, i.e. 20,000 INHABITANTS. There is one loophole clause — if such a collection of habitations contains an Anglican Cathedral, it is a 'city' independent of size.

clapped out: 'After lugging my baggage from one airline counter to another for two hours, I was totally clapped out (EXHAUSTED).'

clean your shoes: a chorus dinned unceasingly into my ears. It doesn't mean to scrape the dirt off or even to saddle-soap them. To clean one's shoes, is to POLISH THEM. (see: *clean your teeth*)

clean your teeth: a command often honored in the breach by youngsters of any western nation. Such cleaning is done with a toothbrush. BRUSH YOUR TEETH. (see: *clean your shoes*)

clerk: means clerk, pronounced clark. He/She could be a Town Clerk, a most important post, the office manager for a city. Alternatively, this could refer to a salesclerk, or a bookkeeper. (see: *salesclerk*)

clobber: Your clobber is what you wear. Some wear flash clobber and others wear more conservative CLOTHING. Depending on the context, this can also refer to violence, either direct as: 'then I clobbered him with a crank handle', or indirect as: 'then the Judge clobbered me with a stiff fine'. Alternatively, the term is often used as we would use 'all this stuff', as 'how will I ever move all this clobber into that little room?' (see: *flash*)

clot: A clot is an individual whom you might uncharitably describe as a dumb CLOD. (see: *berk*)

clothesgrips, or **clothes pegs:** CLOTHESPINS. You must admit that they make more sense than we do. (see: *hair grips or hair clips*)

cobber: My cobber is my FRIEND. (see: *mate*)

cocky: (A) a cocky is a New Zealand FARMER. These come in several varieties: cow cockies (ranchers) tend to be the only ones who rate a modifier to the cocky, but there are also men who you could describe as sheep cockies, dairying cockies, horticultural cockies and mixed cockies. A Kiwi would, however, leave off the descriptive words for all but the cow cockies. (see: *sheep, primary products, high country station, station, dogs, fencing*)

(B) a COCKATOO. This is a parrot sized, white feathered, yellow crested, bird with a disconcerting habit of addressing you in English. Such immortal phrases as 'Cocky wants a peanut' and 'Cocky wants a cup of tea', come to mind. I've often been tempted to honor that last bird's request and see what happens.

*coconut: In addition to referring to the usual hairy milk filled nut, this appellation is used as a derisive name for Pacific Islanders living in New Zealand. The term is most often used by Maoris who resent the Islanders' attempts to move into the jobs and neighborhoods that are their customary reserve. (see: *bong, wog, choppers*)

college: This is not a term that (with 1½ exceptions) refers to University level institutions, nor does it (as in some British and North American institutions) refer to the component parts of a University. These parts are called Faculties, e.g. the Faculties of Medicine and Law. Most colleges are HIGH SCHOOLS and this is the general term for a high school. The institutions that train teachers are also called Teachers' Colleges. These do not give a Bachelor's degree, but rather award a Teaching Diploma. The only remaining 'college' that awards the Bachelor's degree is Lincoln (the exception noted above) Agricultural College. Massey University is still known as Massey College to some old-timers who remember it as an Agricultural college. (see: *Uni, varsity, Teachers College, school, P.P.T.A., false friends*)

collywobbles: A nervous upset stomach. 'Before exams, I always get the collywobbles'.

colonial goose: If fowl is New Zealand's most expensive meat, mutton (which you might think is lamb overseas) is the cheapest. Hence a ROLL OF MUTTON filled WITH A BREADCRUMB STUFFING is substituted. (see: *chook*)

come a greaser — come a gutser: (A) HAVE BAD LUCK (of any kind)

(B) To FALL OFF as from a bike, skis, etc. (see: *can off, bike*)

come again: Kindly REPEAT your statement. It is not improbable that your North American accent and idioms will elicit this request from Kiwis on occasion, although you will find that thanks to TV they are acquainted with most American word usage even if they wouldn't say it that way themselves.

comparisons-differences: There is a tendency to rank order things when comparisons or differences are requested. If you are asked what the differences between North America and New Zealand are, people are usually looking for a conclusion at the end; stating that one or the other is better. Similarly if you ask someone about the differences between, say, the North Island and the South Island, the end of the description will always include a comparative value judgement. Labeling isn't enough, ordering is required.

Concert Chamber: A SMALLish (seats 100-300) HALL used for functions of appropriate size, often but not always musical. (see: *theatre, Town Hall, Opera House, flicks*)

concert programme: The YC radio stations that have news (including the B.B.C. news), symphonic music and readings from intellectual novels. There are also stations with local programming, usually popular music and the X radio stations which are the only ones not owned by the B.C.N.Z. (see: *national programme, B.C.N.Z., wireless*)

concrete yacht: Ever considered building yourself a seagoing yacht? Haven't enough money? Then do as the Kiwis do, pour one. That's right, the art of making concrete yachts originated in New Zealand and is still widely practiced. I'm told that the results float well, are nearly maintenance free and are one whale of a lot cheaper than other construction methods for large yachts. So there! (see: *(Hamilton) jet boat*)

convert a car: In this genteel society, 'down under' one does not do anything so crass as to STEAL A CAR, one merely converts it to one's own use.

cookie: 'What's that you say? Ah! you mean a CUPCAKE. Sorry mate! Fancy food like that is rare, have a piece of pav. instead.' As the influence of Cookie Bear and United States television spreads, more and more people are coming to understand that cookie really means biscuit (cookie to you). (see: *biscuit, pavlova*)

Cookie Bear: New Zealand's version of the 'Jolly Green Giant', only this one wears a bear suit and sells *Hudson's* cookies (Ho! Ho! Ho!). Actually I'm very fond of Cookie Bear, not to mention his cookies. (see: *cookie, biscuit*)

coolibah: An Australian term perverted to unnecessary commercial use. The same meaning as (see:) CHILLY BIN.

copper (the): 'Mum is out back in the washhouse heating up the copper. There is a load of nappies with a new baby, you know.' A large (usually approx. 20 inches in diameter by 15 inches deep) round WASHTUB formerly (and in some households, presently) used to boil up washing water, soap, and clothing which were then agitated with a 'hand operated' wooden paddle. Heating was usually provided by burning wood or coal on a grate under the copper. Most homes 20 or more years old have a washhouse behind them with built in copper, grate and firepot. Today, coppers are often found highly polished and varnished, in living rooms, holding firewood or plants. (see: *mum, washhouse, nappies*).

cordial: a concentrated bottle of liquid flavour essence. A tablespoonful with cold water makes a sweet-flavored drink, popular with children's sweet teeth. Some cordials (particularly lemon) are considered therapeutic for colds, others act as a painless way of increasing vitamin (especially vitamin C) intake. (see: *lemonade*)

corker: 'She's a corker'. Meaning that the subject under discussion (not necessarily female, see: *she*) is VERY, VERY GOOD indeed.

corn: Not necessarily those yellow bits on the cob. This is a term referring to GRAIN of any kind. (see: *maize, false friends*)

corned silverside or corned brisket (lower quality): CORNED BEEF; not like your local delicatessen. For one thing it is much cheaper and for another, it comes in roast-like chunks rather than paper-thin slices, but the taste is easily the equal of the beef you corn yourself. You will enjoy this very much provided you have been away from the corner deli for no less than four months. (see: *delicatessen*)

cornflour: when your cookbook says CORNSTARCH, use cornflour. This isn't masa. (see: *cassia, cinnamon*)

cot: a cot is an infant's CRIB. (see: *crib*)

cotton: This is what you use to sew up that tear in your frock or trousers. A needle and cotton instead of a needle and THREAD. The word is also used for garments made of the boll weevil's favorite munch. (see: *ball frock*)

country service: In order to be eligible for promotion beyond basic levels of pay, public school teachers under 30 years of age must spend three years teaching at schools considered rural. If they are over 30 this requirement disappears. Some of these are a reasonable driving distance from cities, or even located in good sized towns; others are the one teacher primary school of little red schoolhouse fame and two years of this is equal to the three otherwise required. Some people decide they like the life and never come back from country service. After all, you can find yourself the community's intellectual leader plus being the family with the tennis court, swimming pool and possibly library, since a house is provided in these isolated jobs and it has access to all the school's facilities.

courgette: A gorgeous little ZUCCHINI. (see: *veges, capsicum, swedes, aubergine*)

cove: (A) 'He's a right rum cove, that bartender', translates as he's a very peculiar PERSON, that bartender.

  (B) An INLET. (see: *false friends*)

cow pat: Not a bovine caress. (see: *manure*)

cracker: (A). SOMETHING really GOOD. 'She's a cracker', is high praise for any non-male person, object, animal, or event. (see: *corker, she, false friends*)

  (B). A Christmas cracker is a 3″ long cylinder covered with crepe paper that is twisted at both ends. It is traditional at Christmas dinners to share one of these with a friend. You each take hold of one of the twisted ends and pull. The result is a bang (from a gunpowder charge approximately equal to that in a cap pistol) and a prize reminiscent of those found in cereal cartons.

crate: teenage slang for the most prominent feature(s) of a buxom wench. (also: old car, wooden box etc.) (see: *charlies, lusty wench, town bike, scrubber*)

cream: comes in only one version in New Zealand. The N.Z. version is the equivalent of double cream or WHIPPING CREAM in the U.S. If you want something lighter you'll have to ask for (see:) *top of the milk*. A warning, Kiwis normally drink their coffee with milk in it rather than cream. If you want cream you must ask for it. If you like your tea black you must ask for that. (see: *tea*)

creche: (A) A COMMUNITY NURSERY for babes in arms.

    (B) A NATIVITY SCENE. (see: *kindy, playcentre*)

crib: House of ... No, sorry. This term refers to a weekend cottage in South Island parlance. (see: *bach, cot*)

crikey Dick — cripes: GOOD LORD! Possibly a reference to Dick Seddon, a prominent Liberal Party (later to become the Labour Party) Prime Minister (1893-1906) of New Zealand. (a.k.a. King Dick). (see: *Labour Party, Prime Minister*)

crim: A crim is a CRIMINAL, this term is used by police, social workers, prison officers, criminals, etc.

crook or **gone crook:** If you are talking about an inanimate object, it is NOT WORKING well; an organic one is SICK or ANGRY. 'Jim was feeling crook (sick) when he drove home last night and it didn't help that his engine went crook (broke down) half-way there. He sure went crook (got angry with, berated) his wife when he got home, for not taking the bucket of bolts into the garage as she had promised.' (see: *bucket of bolts*)

crooked as a dog's hind leg: Some of the back metal roads in the mountains of central Otago (e.g. Crown Range Road) could be safely described this way. It is seldom used as a reflection on someone's honesty. ZIGZAG. (see: *metal, Otago*)

crossed cheques: If you write a CHECK on a New Zealand bank and you wish it to be FOR DEPOSIT ONLY, then you should draw two parallel lines slanting slightly off the vertical across the lettering at the top of the check, e.g.

    Bank of New Zealand
    Corner George and Pitt Streets
    Dunedin North, Dunedin, N.Z.

If someone gives you such a check you cannot legally cash it or endorse it to someone else, you can only deposit it in your own account. These crossed lines override the words 'or bearer' which appear after the 'Pay' blank on all N.Z. checks. Most Americans in N.Z. tend to cross out the 'or bearer' thus making it on the face like a U.S. check. As far as I know the legal validity of this practice has not been tested. (see: *words*)

crumpet: sold commercially, this version of an ENGLISH MUFFIN (the batter is somewhat more liquid) resembles a thick dollar pancake on one side and a Swiss cheese on the other. They are just the right size to fit into your toaster. These can be found in the shops during the colder (April-November) months only. (see: (a) *bit of crumpet*)

crutch — crutching: The crutch is the GROIN and crutching is the removal of fecal matter adhering to this area of sheep. (see: *dag, short and curlies, minge*)

cuda: a cute cuddly name for a BARRACUDA! (see: *white pointer*)

cup: as 'a cup of flour' in a cookbook recipe is a standard 8 oz. cup but in the recipe you got from the lady next door, is usually a teacup. (see: *tablespoon*)

cuppa: A CUP OF TEA or coffee. 'Have a cuppa' is a friendly neighborly greeting repeated thousands of times a day throughout New Zealand.

curley cues: Ugly to look at and sometimes painful to use, these are OLD-FASHIONED HAIR CURLERS.

curling: *A game* brought over to Central Otago from Scotland. It's a bit like shuffleboard on ice, except that you use 40 lb elipsoids of stone equipped with a goosenecked handle and a man with a long-handled broom moves nimbly in front of the moving curling stone clearing the path and effectively guiding the onrushing boulder. This was an Olympic sport as late as 1932 (I don't know about more recent Winter Olympics). (see: *hockey*)

cushy job: What most of us think the other guy has, an EASY (cushioned) JOB. (see: CENSORED!)

cyclostyle: 'Barry, please ask your secretary to cyclostyle these two notices, *cellotape* them together and use *drawing pins* to put them up all over the factory.

'Barry, please ask your secretary to MIMEOGRAPH these notices, *Scotch Tape* them together and use thumb tacks to . . .' (see: *cellotape, drawing pins*)

D

dag: literally, this refers to a clot of FECAL MATTER sticking to the tail end of a sheep. It has, however, become part of the language as in 'What a dag!' — an admiring statement directed at someone who has done something slightly risque. Some joker threw a pie in the Prime Minister's face, what a dag! (see: *Fred Dagg, joker, rattle your dags, crutch, crutching*). p.s. Somebody really did.

dairy: a NEIGHBORHOOD mom and pop STORE. It will typically sell dairy products, canned goods, fresh vegetables, ice cream cones, magazines, newspapers and paperbacks. This store is usually open seven days a week and often 14 hours a day. Many young couples get their first stake to start a business by running one of these for a couple of years. (see: *milk treatment station, milk shed*)

Dallies: New Zealanders whose forebears came from Dalmatia in what is now Yugoslavia. The Dallies are concentrated in the North of the North Island and tend to be farmers and winemakers.

Darby and Joan: The ARCHETYPAL, happily married ELDERLY COUPLE. They've been together so long they not only think alike, they look alike. Fibber McGee and Molly without the closet. They were the subjects of a ballad written by Henry Woodfall in 18th century England. The ballad is long forgotten by the general public but the phrase Darby and Joan is instantly recognizable and understood by any Kiwi.

date: 1/2/84 in the United States implies the 2nd January 1984. In New Zealand, it implies 1st February 1984. That is, the month precedes the day in the United States and follows it in New Zealand. (see: *false friends, backwards*)

dear: EXPENSIVE. Fillet mignon at $2.40 lb. is very dear, or wouldn't you agree?

decimalization: On the 10th of July 1967, New Zealand went from a pounds (£), *shillings (s) pence (d) system to a dollars ($) and cents (c) system. Everyone has adjusted very well by now, but you will hear the older terms still used, especially for very expensive purchases. (see: bob, shilling, pound, sixpence, penny, metrication*)

dekko: Probably picked up, like a lot of other things, on the Indian sub-continent by troops of the British 'Raj'; it was originally a Hindu word. 'Let's take a dekko at that new car.' Let's take a look at that new car. (see: *shufti, squiz*)

delicatessen: It ain't kosher, there is no chopped liver, pastrami, lox or smoked whitefish and the quality of much of what is there leaves much to be desired. By local standards, it is dear. (see: *dear*)

destructor: A *small closed stove* usually located in the kitchens of older homes and used to dispose of any burnable waste. (see: *wetback destructor*)

dial: 'If you don't behave, I'll wipe your dial (bash your FACE) for you.' (see: *knuckle sandwich, face re-arranged*)

diddle: 'He diddled her out of her life savings.' He SWINDLED. . .

(oh) diddums: (A) affectionate babytalk when talking to a baby.

(B) a heavily SARCASTIC expression of sympathy when addressed to an adult. 'Oh diddums, did you really lose all your money at the races yesterday? If you had taken me to the beach instead, *as you promised(!)* it wouldn't have happened, would it?'

differences: (see: *comparisons — differences*)

dim sims: Chinese MEATBALLS rolled IN BATTER and sold in the ubiquitous fish and chip shops. (see: *fish and chips, pie-cart*)

Dinkie: A beautician's metal clip is used for holding back HAIR. It is similar in shape to an alligator CLIP.

dinner: a word infrequently heard. You will, however, be understood if you use it. A very special afternoon or evening meal as Christmas Dinner. (see: *tea, supper*)

dipped out: 'Trev (Trevor) dipped out on his driving test'. FAILED.

do a Hollywood: For those folks who come from the Los Angeles area, it won't surprise you that this term means TO EXAGGERATE. It usually refers to the histrionic exaggeration of an injury on the playing field. (see: *do your bun, throw a wobbly*)

do the ton: DRIVE a self propelled petrol powered vehicle in excess of 100 MILES PER HOUR.

Do you think it would pass in a crowd? IS THIS thing I have (made, built, cooked or possibly bought) ANY GOOD? (see: *just like a bought one*)

do your bun or do your scone: is to BLOW YOUR FUSE. This, is a temper trantrum but is less general and more directional than to throw a wobbly. One does one's bun at someone. These terms are more often used for adults while children are more likely to throw a wobbly. (see: *throw a* *wobbly*)

docket: is an INVOICE.

dog ranger: Sounds exotic, doesn't it, a cross between Lassie and a Texas Ranger. Unfortunately, this employee of the Society for the Prevention of Cruelty to Animals is the local DOG CATCHER. This can be a somewhat more important job in a pastoral economy than in an industrial one, as loose dogs can harry and kill sheep, and there are sheep everywhere. (see: *dogs, huntaway, strong-eyed bitch, sheep*)

(the) **dog that bit you:** HAIR OF THE DOG.

dog trials: New Zealand's superbly trained sheep-herding DOGS and their trainers get to strut their stuff at these rural COMPETITIONS. A common task is for a dog to go to a hill three or four hundred yards way, go to the far side of the hill (where his trainer can't see him), collect a small flock of five or six sheep, bring them back to a pen next to the trainer, and put them in the pen. The trainer is allowed to whistle, gesture and close the pen gate. This is something you must see to appreciate. Highly recommended! (see: *dogs, huntaway, strong-eyed bitch*)

dogs: To most North Americans a dog is a friendly tail-wagging pet. To most Kiwis, a dog is a WORKING ANIMAL, an integral part of a farm's equipment and has no more place in your house than does a horse or a tractor. Immigrants from Britain don't feel this way. Usually, the first thing they do, unless it is to go right home, is to buy a large dog as a pet. Something they couldn't have coped with in London. The attitudes of some urban Kiwis have likewise begun to change, but very slowly. This change is not necessarily desirable, as loose dogs in rural or semi-rural areas (most of New Zealand) can be an economic menace. (see: *dog ranger, poms, huntaway, strong-eyed bitch, get in behind, alsatian*)

dog's breakfast: an UNHOLY MESS, e.g. my office.

dole: Four years ago, I wrote:

'In a country that prides itself on being a highly socialistic welfare state, it shouldn't be difficult to get on *relief*, but this country also rarely has over 1% unemployment, so to get on the dole you need a really good reason as to why you are incapable of working, since work is usually freely available. A solo parent of very young children would qualify.'

Alas, those days are gone, unemployment plus special work (even by the government's very conservative method of calculation) runs around 6% (1979) and government-sponsored make-work schemes abound. Young people for the first time in the last 10 years have to scratch for jobs upon High School or University graduation and can no longer assume they have their choice. This is a hard adjustment to make when it happens all of a sudden to you. Older folk hark back to the 30's and say, 'it isn't as bad as that, yet!' (see: (government) *special work, solo parent, family benefit*)

domain: a domain is a locally administered PARK usually in the COUNTRY. (see: *park, reserve*)

domes: The SNAPS that you commonly find on garments in North America and don't find in some expected places in New Zealand. Would you believe pajama flies? (see: *cotton, haberdashery*)

done in: BEAT, tired.

done your chips: 'You've done your chips'. You've FAILED. What a useful expression this would be in Las Vegas, Monte Carlo or Tasmania. (see: *blow it*)

don't come the raw prawn with me: DON'T TRY TO FEED ME THAT LINE. (see: *prawn*)

doorstops: This is what my Kiwi friends call the perfectly ordinary AMERICAN SANDWICHES that I cobble together. These are by no means dagwoods, but compared to a New Zealand sandwich (e.g. one slice of bread, half normal thickness, buttered and rolled around two thin slices of cucumber or one stick of asparagus), they are enormous. (see: *sandwich*)

double: When placing a long-distance telephone call in New Zealand, or any other circumstance in which you are giving a telephone number, and that number has two recurring digits, e.g. 78846, you must say, seven, double eight, four six, rather than seven, eight, eight, four six. Otherwise, you are in danger of being misunderstood and told that your have left out a number (the second 8).

down the road: IN THE FUTURE. 'That job is down the road.'

down trou: The ceremonial SELF-REMOVAL OF A MALE'S LOWER GARMENTS, often while standing on a table in a crowded bar so as to afford a view to the widest possible public. This is usually enhanced by choosing Saturday night for the activity. An activity sanctioned by tradition and alcohol, its practitioners are usually in their late teens or early twenties and in a bar largely patronized by their peers. (see: *berko, drop your tweeds, [to] take the mickey*)

drapers — drapery: Well, you can get drapes there but that's an understatement; a draper is a DRY GOODS STORE. Clothes, sheets, towels, material, buttons and bows etc. (see: *manchester, mercers*)

draughts: Have you ever seen two old men sitting in the park playing draughts? Well, if you have, you patronize different parks than I do, but that's the way the story goes. Draughts are CHECKERS.

drawing pins: THUMBTACKS (see: *cyclostyle, cellotape*)

drench: To drench a sheep or cow does not mean to dump them in a vat of something. Instead, a man, with a tank on his back connected by a hose to a waterpistol-like device in his hands, grabs each animal, shoves the pistol down his throat and shoots in a dose of medicine. (see: *sheep, false friends*)

Dress Circle: Remember sitting in the cheap BALCONY seats in your local movie theater as a kid? A little popcorn for the people below and/or a little slap and tickle with your date? Well, in New Zealand these same seats are the expensive seats with plush seat coverings and not frequented by children or adolescents (except on first dates). It is the downstairs seats that serve the same social and economic groups in New Zealand that sit in the balcony in the United States. (see: *flicks, slap and tickle, backwards*)

dressed pie: A (approx. 4 inch diameter) MEAT PIE that has a crust DECORATED WITH PEAS, beetroot and mashed potatoes (see: *meat pie, mince pie; pea, pie and pud, pie cart*)

dressing gown: BATHROBE.

drive you crackers: 'That amplified music will drive you crackers.' That amplified music will DRIVE YOU CRAZY. (see: *bonkers*)

driving: If you are right-handed and you ride your horse ON THE LEFT-hand-side of the road, then your sword arm is in the best position to engage oncoming traffic. New Zealand, Australia, England, Japan, Cyprus, Jersey, Kenya, Malaysia, Malta, Mauritius, Mozambique, Surinam, Tanzania, Thailand, Uganda, Rhodesia, South Africa (etc.?) have taken precautions against the day that the horse and sword return. You will find that your reflexes cope quite well until you have to make a right turn. Then the training of many years will probably put you in the wrong lane. Expect to be a bloody menace for 3-5 days while you retrain yourself. One more problem, you will continuously find yourself arriving at the left hand door of the car you plan to drive. This would be fine but the steering wheel is on the other side. (see: *walking, quite, bloody, backwards*)

drongo: A DRIP. This refers to people, not plumbing.

drop kick: a FIELD GOAL ATTEMPT in rugby.

drop your tweeds: (see: DOWN TROU)

drying green: There are bowling greens, golf greens and then there is the PLACE WHERE YOU HAVE ERECTED YOUR CLOTHESLINE. (see: *bowling*)

duchesse: The hereditary New Zealand title for a LOW CHEST OF DRAWERS WITH A MIRROR on it so it can double as a dressing table. (see: *lowboy, tallboy*)

duck dive: To dive like a duck, i.e. SURFACE DIVE. (see: *honey pot-bomb, belly buster*)

duck itch: a RASH that develops as a result of contact with a waterborne parasite that infests some of New Zealand's southern lakes. It has just left its snail host and is looking for a duck to grow up in. Look for warning signs.

duck shoving: 'I'm sorry, madam, this office does not deal with your problem — you have to go to the under-clerk's office two miles in that direction . . .'

'I'm sorry, madam, this office does deal with your type of problem but your specific problem is a special case and you have to go to the under-under-clerk's office, 2½ miles in that direction . . .'

'Yes, madam, you are in the right place, but you should have come earlier, it is 4:31 p.m. and we are closed . . .'

'Good morning, madam, can I help you . . .'

'I'm sorry, madam, our Mr Campbell handles these things and he is on his annual fortnight's vacation. You should have come yesterday.'

PASSING THE BUCK. (see: *fortnight*)

dummy: a baby's PACIFIER; also FOOL. (see: *clot*)

Dundee cake: A FRUIT CAKE only lightly speckled with fruit.

dunny: (see: TOILET, toilet paper, loo, bog, grot, lav.)

duplicate bridge: The boards are made of board but the rules are the same and you are more than welcome at any club. If you want to meet some Kiwis, I recommend this method.

duster: When you were a kid did your teacher ever give you the job of taking the BLACKBOARD ERASERS outside and beating them together creating great interesting clouds of chalk dust? Things are no different in New Zealand, except they are called dusters. This term is also used for dustcloths.

dustman: the man who collects the garbage bins (the GARBAGE COLLECTOR), usually at a dead run, since the job pays, not by the hour but rather a fixed number of streets must be covered. As a result of working at this accelerated pace, they are usually finished between noon and one o'clock (starting at 8.00 a.m.) Some hopeful authors have found this a healthy job that allows them time to write while surviving. Others find it provides more time for their own homes or for drinking with their mates.

dux: from the Latin dux, meaning leader or guide. This is the title given to the top scholar of the top class (7th form) in a high school; he is the equivalent of the American High School VALEDICTORIAN.

E

ear bashing: This enterprise is traditionally accomplished with tongue and tonsils rather than fists, but is no less painful for all that. Ear bashings range from a bollicking to anyone riding his favorite hobbyhorse. TALKING TO EXCESS. (see: *bollicking, ear wagging*)

ear wagging: a gentler (see:) *ear bashing*. Often used to refer to NAGGING it can also refer to any RUNNING OFF AT THE MOUTH.

easies: GIRDLE.

East Coast-Gisborne: The area known as the East Coast is smaller than that known as Gisborne but is totally enclosed within it. It consists of the peninsula that forms the northeastern bulge of the North Island plus the area immediately inland from that bulge. Statistics (1976) below apply to East coast only. Population 48,147 homo sapiens, 3,403,000 ovis aries (baa) and 464,000 bos taurus (moo). Spectacular scenery around East Cape, beautiful empty beaches, and the motorcamp in Gisborne includes the old jail, whose cells you can occupy for a small fee. The major metropolitan area surrounds and includes the city of Gisborne, 30,4000 pop. (see: *North Island*)

eh: (pronounced as 'ay' in 'hay') Used as ʻDON'T YOU AGREE?ʼ e.g. Hot today, (over 50°F), eh? Frequency of use decreases with years of schooling and increases as you go north, reaching a maximum in the Auckland area. It may come from the Maori word, ei.

eiderdown: a FEATHER filled QUILT. New Zealand is well known among aficionados for its down-filled sleeping-bags. These quilts are made by the same people and are very popular in a country where many consider it unhealthy to heat bedrooms at any time of the year. (see: *central heating*)

11's es: an adopted English custom, practised by a very limited proportion of the population. SOCIAL DRINKS ON SUNDAY MORNING.

English sunbathing: The risky and risque exposure of one's ankles (possibly even the whole leg below the knee) to the rays of the sun while ensuring the rest of one's body is swathed in thick layers of woollen clothing. I suspect it has something to do with the English climate, but it does take newly arrived poms some time to adjust. (see: *pom*)

entree: This is the COURSE BETWEEN the SOUP AND the MAIN COURSE. Somehow in the United States, the term main course has disappeared and entree has taken its place. Entree means entrance, so the name makes more sense in New Zealand than it does in the United States.

eryaguan: 'Eryaguan mate? Beaut day. Let's go'n (go and) sink a few'. HOW ARE YOU going (doing) . . . (see: *owsidguan, gidday, mate, beaut, sink a few*)

F

face flannel: a FACE CLOTH. You probably won't find one of these in your hotel room, nor will your host be likely to issue you one, should you stay in a private home although both will be lavish with various kinds of towels. It's not that they aren't used in New Zealand, because they are. I can only speculate that it's like a toothbrush, so intimate an item that you are expected to carry your own.

(to get your) face re-arranged: an offer occasionally made in the heat of an argument. The re-arrangement is accomplished using a closed fist as a tool. (see: *dial, knuckle sandwich*)

Faculty: In the U.S. the faculty of a university consists of the teaching personnel. In N.Z. universities are divided into subdivisions called faculties which correspond to those called COLLEGES in the U.S. For example the Faculty of Arts and Music, the Faculty of Science, the Faculty of Medicine, etc. The teachers are referred to as the staff or academic staff. (see: *Uni, varsity, college, false friends*)

fair dinkum: This one is a loan from the Aussies and means 'IT'S REALLY TRUE', or 'IS IT REALLY TRUE?' depending on context. (see: *Aussie*)

fair go: A fair go is a FAIR CHANCE. There is even a T.V. program, with this name, devoted to redressing the wrongs suffered by individuals at the hands of businesses or government. (see: *gizago, ombudsman*)

false friends: These probably don't mean what you think they do. (see:)

air conditioning	*bowling*
Associate Professor	*bubble*
award	*bushwacker*
bastard	*cane*
bathroom	*canoe*
be away laughing	*Chair*
Belgium	*cheek*
bike	*cheeks*
billion	*cheerios*
bird	*chippies*
biscuit	*cinnamon*
bloody	*college*
bog	*come again*
bonnet	*comparisons*
boot	*copper*

37

corn	physician
cot	prawn
cotton	privates
cove	proms
cracker	punter
crib	punting
crook	quite
Dairy	range
differences	reader
drench	ring
entree	root
fanny	rubber
fencing	scoff
flaming	skip
flash	sister
flat	sixpence
flog	sod
football	solicitor
freezer	spider
gallon	station
gallops	stone
girdle	strides
globe	stuff
guts	straight away
hard case	Sunday papers
hockey	suspenders
homely	swept up
honours	swish
hooker	tablespoon
hot dogs	T-bone
house	television licence
hurray	thanks
Lecturer	tip
lemonade	togs
lift	toot
lusty wench	trots
manure	You shouldn't have done that
match	vacuum tube
mate	valve
matron	varsity
mean	villa
messages	wardrobe
mighty	wetback
misunderstanding	wetback destructor
naughty	white pointer
Normal school	wicked
not really	wops
period	

family benefit: New Zealand PAYS its residents FOR HAVING CHILDREN. This isn't the stated intent of the law which is designed to ensure that there are funds for the necessities of life for a child but it is the effect. Every child resident in New Zealand is in receipt (via his parents) of a stipend which can be collected in instalments or 'capitalized' to the tune of about $3,000 for the downpayment on a house.

fancy: 'I fancy that bird'. I LIKE (WANT, DESIRE) that girl. (see: *bird, got tickets on*)

**fanny: One of the no-no words. This refers specifically to the FEMALE EXTERNAL GENITALIA. People will be very shocked if you talk about patting someone on the fanny. Use backside or bum instead, but not fanny!

I'll never forget the first time I used that perfectly ordinary phrase while lecturing to 250 University freshmen. The shocked silence that greeted my 'humorous' sally puzzled me until I was able to ask a friend shortly after the lecture. It did give me a red face and a peg on which to hang the next lecture on cultural relativism. (see: *backside, bum*)

*fart arsing around: GOOFING OFF. (see: *puddle around, muck around*)

Father Christmas: You know, that jolly old man with the red suit, 12 tiny reindeer etc. Elsewhere he may be St Nicholas, or SANTA CLAUS. In New Zealand he is Father Christmas. Perhaps this is recognition of the usual proximate source of those wee guifties. (see: *Christmas, wee*)

Father's Day: The FIRST SUNDAY IN SEPTEMBER as contrasted with the first Sunday in June in the U.S. Mother's Day is the same in both countries (2nd Sunday in May). My dad got a shock when telegraphed a Father's Day greeting in the September of my first year in N.Z. I got a bit of culture shock in return when his reply informed me that it wasn't Father's Day in the U.S.

Fed up to the back teeth: Did you ever wonder where one was *fed up* to?

Feed *Moose*: A sign prevalent on New Zealand roadsides. *Moose* is the name of an ANIMAL FEED. Evidence indicates that there are no living wild moose in New Zealand although some were introduced into Fiordland early this century. They don't seem to have adapted. (see: PEERLESS SHEEP NUTS)

fencing: (A) One of the most highly skilled and physically demanding jobs on a New Zealand farm is SINKING FENCEPOSTS AND STRINGING FENCING WIRE. In fact, there are individuals and firms that specialize in this, but every cocky has occasion to do some of his own fencing.

(B) Don't let me mislead you, as with every other sport except gridiron, there is an active federation of clubs in New Zealand that fences with foils rather than hammers, nails and wire strainers. (see: *cocky, gridiron, primary products, false friends*)

filled roll: A SANDWICH usually made from a hot dog or hamburger bun. It invariably includes a slice of red beet, potted meat and lettuce. Unless you are fond of beets, try something else. (see: *beetroot, bread roll*)

fillet: pronounced 'fill it' – it means the same as the word you pronounce 'fill eh'. (see: *T-bone, butchery*)

Fiordland: The west coast of Southland. An area carved with fiords as spectacular as any in Norway. Unless you take a special yacht trip around this coast it is only really accessible at two points, from Manapouri, where you will also see the power station buried deep in a mountain and looking like a 'Star Wars' set, and from Milford Sound, the terminus of the Milford track. (see: *Southland, Otago, South Island*)

fire: coal, wood, gas and electric. The tricky one is the last. An ELECTRIC HEATER is called an electric fire and the adjective is often left off. (see: *torch*)

fish and chips: Breaded and battered fillets of fish deep fried and accompanied by an order of french fries, all served up (to go) wrapped in a piece of newspaper or, recently, brown paper. Traditionally one does not open the package but rather tears off a corner and (preserving the heat) burrows in, like a worm into an apple, eating each delicious morsel as your fingers reach it. Cheap, inelegant and usually very good, this takes the place of an American's hamburger and fries. It is, in my opinion, generally better than the latter. It is always better than the local hamburger and chips! (see: *hamburgers, hot dog, chips, shark and tatties, greasies*)

fit as a trout: 'Old Sam is as fit as a trout, he walked five miles yesterday just to sink a few with me.' Old Sam is IN GOOD SHAPE, he walked five miles yesterday just to drink a few beers with me.' (see: *sink a few*)

fizzler: 'It's a fizzler!' It's a FAILURE. As are most things that fizzle out.

fizzy drink: A SOFT DRINK is a fizzy drink. Rather more descriptive isn't it? (see: *lemonade*)

flagon: A HALF imperial GALLON BOTTLE OF BEER. (Now 2.25 liters). It is customary to buy a couple of flagons from the bottle store to take home; much as an American might pick up a six pack. (see: *gallon, half g, bottle store, beer, pissed*)

flake: as in 'flake out'. Go to SLEEP.

flaming: means DAMN. 'Sam's a flaming bore'. 'Then the flaming tire went flat'. 'Where were you the whole flaming day?' Let's see, something that is damned goes to hell. Hell (except for Dante's bottom floor) is a very hot, even flaming place. Cussing at one remove. (see: *ruddy, bloody*)

flash: (from flashy but without the negative connotations). EXPENSIVE – ELEGANT. 'That's a flash restaurant'. **Dead flash** is the superlative of flash. A MOST or VERY flash place. If a bar has carpet on the floor, it earns this appellation. It also refers to an activity traditionally practiced by otherwise naked men in raincoats. (see: *swept up, swish*)

flat: The shape of the earth before the discovery of New Zealand. Use this term instead of APARTMENT. Apartment is a chic word that no-one ever uses in casual conversations. Friends who live in the Jerningham Apartments (a high-rise co-op. and one of the 'in' places in Wellington) always say that they 'have a flat in the Jerningham Apartments'. (see: *false friends*)

flicks or (less commonly) **flea house:** The MOVIES (some move, some flicker). One generally books (reserves) a seat and dresses in one's best, especially on Friday or Saturday night. The best seats are in the dress circle, (balcony). With some exceptions, this is not a theater. Theaters serve another purpose.

The movies are subject to censorship by a governmental agency in N.Z. The resulting bowdlerized versions are then classified as follows:

G — 'General Exhibition' (e.g. Bambi)

GY — 'Recommended for persons 13 and over' (e.g. Ben Hur, Star Wars)

GA — 'Recommended as suitable for adults only (e.g. Jaws)

The above classifications do not have the force of law. The following classifications do have the force of law, and both the theater proprietor and the minor concerned are liable to prosecution for violation.

R — Restricted

R13 — Only persons over 13 years of age admitted

R16 — Only persons over 16 years of age admitted

R18 — Only persons over 18 years of age admitted

R20 — Only persons over 20 years of age admitted

(see: *Patricia Bartlett, X-rated, dress circle, theatre, Opera House, Concert Chamber, Town Hall*)

flog: To STEAL or to SELL. A salesman may flog (sell) you a car while a thief may flog (steal) the hubcaps. Theft is comparatively rare in New Zealand — some makes of motor vehicle (like mine) don't even have locks on their doors.

fly cemeteries — dead fly biscuits — raisin biscuits: a very thin flat cookie that comes in sheets and appears to be 90% fruit and 10% pastry — good but gooey. (see: *biscuit, scone, cookie, Fruit Fingers*)

F.O.L.: New Zealand's version of the A.F.L.-C.I.O. (American Federation of Labor-Congress of Industrial Organizations) or the British T.U.C. (Trades Union Congress). The Kiwi version is called the FEDERATION OF LABOUR, and has as its members the multiplicity of unions that represent and control the New Zealand work force outside of Government service. (see: *P.S.A.*) What power struggles there are, appear, to an outside observer, to be between the F.O.L. and the Government. Employers, while attempting to influence both sides, in effect appear to accept the decision of these two major power brokers. New Zealand operates a closed shop system so that most people must belong to unions in order to work. The present (1978) government is trying to introduce the open shop system but best of British to them. (see: *best of British, industrial unrest, industrial action, union bashing, freezing workers, wharfies*).

football, or **footie:** SOCCER, in which you can use anything but your hands, i.e. feet, shoulders, head. Ball resembles a basketball and rules resemble hockey. The term more often refers to RUGBY FOOTBALL played by usual rules (whatever they are), Rugby Union rules, or Australian rules, all of which resemble our football without the protective clothing. We don't play football, we play gridiron. (see *gridiron, wall Blacks, try, false friends*)

footpath: The part of the roadway intended for feet; the SIDEWALK. (see: *walking, kerb*)

fortnight: You probably know (if you read historical novels) that this is an archaic term for a period of TWO WEEKS. What is hard to realize is that this word is part of the living everyday language in New Zealand, used, without exception, in place of saying two weeks. If you think it is strange to hear, wait until you use it for the first time, nervously awaiting the incredulous laughter that never comes.

fossick — fossick about: to SEARCH for or look for something. 'I'll go fossick about in that rubbish heap I call an office, and see if I can find those papers for you'. (see: *rubbish*)

4 and a half: GALLONS OF BEER in a metal keg, available from your local hotel. Enough for yourself and one or two mates. For a real thirst rent a mini-tanker. (see: *gallon, beer, hotel, mini-tanker*)

(a) 4 x 2: is a 2 X 4 inch piece of wood. Surprising how hard it is to accommodate to this one. (see: *backwards*)

Fred Dagg: New Zealand comedy figure. A STEREOTYPE of the N.Z. FARMER, he is popular with many segments of the community including many of the farmers he characterizes. The role is most often used to lampoon Government figures, political parties and anyone else whose dignity could do with a bit of deflation. (see: *dag, cocky*)

free walk: On at least two of New Zealand's most famous hiking trails (the Routeburn and the Milford track), you can go either by sponsored (escorted) walks or ON YOUR OWN. If you are doing it on your own, you carry your own food, in addition to the rest of your gear, and spend the nights in marginally less comfortable accommodation. On the sponsored walks, the guide carries the food and cooks, you are responsible for carrying only yourself, your sleeping bag, your personal and tourist paraphernalia. (see: *tramping*)

freezer, or **freezing works:** This is the place where New Zealand's major exports are converted from meat on the hoof to fastidiously prepared sides or whole carcases for overseas consumption. A SLAUGHTERHOUSE for export lamb and beef. This is one of the kingpins of the economy and everyone knows it. (see: *freezing workers, abattoir, works, (the) season, primary products, (the) chain, false friends*)

freezing workers: These men and women have one of the hardest, most monotonous and best paid jobs in the country; slaughtering stock for export. For most it is seasonal work, and they work for about nine months and then take a less demanding job for the remainder of the year or just rest up for the next season. The industry is plagued with strikes (called industrial unrest) as the beginning of 'the season' is a point where these workers have the entire nation's prosperity in their hands, and they know it. For most, the money is the only thing that keeps them at this otherwise unrewarding job and any opportunity to sweeten the pot is important. If a farmer has to hold on to stock past optimal slaughtering time it puts on fat; this lowers its value in an industry where U.S. customers (for example) demand lean meat. In addition, the animals waiting for slaughter are eating up the feed being saved for wintering over breeding stock. This means that the farmer must either kill breeding stock, reducing the number of head he will have to sell in the subsequent year, or buy in expensive winter feed from someone who has it to spare. On the other side, the Freezing Works have contracted with shippers to have refrigerator ships (or container ships with capacity for running the containers' cooling systems) pick up the prepared meat on specific dates. If these dates are not met, the ships sail without that portion of their load. This has two effects, firstly when the meat is ready there are no ships to carry it, and secondly it arrives at traditional markets too late for its usual sale (e.g. England for Christmas season dinners). A wharfies' strike can have the same effects on shipment, if not slaughter. (see: *freezer, primary products, traditional markets, wharfies, industrial action,* (the) *British disease,* (the) *season, overseas funds, terms of trade,* (the) *chain, F.O.L.*)

french letter: prophylactic device. (see: *rubber*)

Friesian: During World War I the British Empire (which included New Zealand) was understandably upset with its Teutonic neighbors. One of the consequences of this annoyance was that the large black and white splotched cattle called HOLSTEINS after a German State, were renamed for the Dutch province across the border where they could just as easily have originated. Americans were either not so mad at Germany or, more likely, weaker on geography, and didn't change the name. (see: *Belgium*)

fruit fingers: FIG NEWTONS by any other name do taste as sweet. (see: *fly cemeteries, biscuit, cookie, scone*)

fruit machine: Pull that lĕver (pronounced lēver) and watch the rollers spin; 3 lemons, too bad. A ONE ARMED BANDIT by any other name costs just as much. These are very rare in New Zealand, most people have heard of them but of those who have never been out of the country, very few have seen one. Don't despair though, the T.A.B., the Golden Kiwi, and the Post Office Bonus Bonds will be happy to take your wagers and your money. (see: *T.A.B., Golden Kiwi, Bonus Bonds*)

fruiterer: This is the man who sells you your fresh fruit and vegetables, a FRUIT AND VEGETABLE VENDOR or, as the English would say, GREEN-GROCER. The majority of such vendors in New Zealand are Chinese family businesses, many families having started as market gardeners after the New Zealand goldrush was over. Most of their stores do sell a few things besides fruit and vegetables. For instance, I buy my Chinese whisky at the fruiterers.

full stop: Is what you put at the end of a sentence, a PERIOD, (the punctuation kind). (see: *period*)

G

gallon or **Imperial gallon:** It's bigger than the U.S. gallon (even the variety used in Texas). An Imperial (British Empire) gallon is 1.2 U.S. GALLONS. This means that you are constantly trying to recalculate. Petrol (gas) is $1.95 (Jan 1980) a gallon! Wait a minute, that's bigger than a U.S. gallon, $1.95 ÷ 1.2 = $1.63 per U.S. gallon (still a lot). My mate Barry gets thirty miles a gallon from his bucket of bolts. Let's see, that's 30 ÷ 1.2 = 25 m.p.g. U.S. Good, but not as good as it sounded. Since this definition was written, New Zealand has gone metric and petrol is sold in liters (and discussed in Imperial gallons). The price (Jan 1980) per liter is 43¢, still the equivalent of $1.95 per U.S. gallon. (see: *litre, petrol, metrication, bucket of bolts, false friends*)

gallops: That vulgar variety of HORSE RACING in which the rider actually sits upon the horse. The most popular of the kinds of racing in New Zealand, where racing is one of the most popular past-times. No matter how small, every community seems to have a racetrack although it may only be used once or twice a year. (see: *beer, T.A.B., trots, punter, punting*)

gaol: JAIL, same meaning and pronunciation – different spelling. (see: *nett, programme, 'Words'*)

garden gnome: a PLASTER OF PARIS version of one of the seven DWARFS brightly painted and placed in the front yard for the appreciation of passers-by.

gasbag: An adult (usually female) who releases wind from her lungs, vibrating the vocal chords, during a large proportion of each day; a CHATTERBOX.

G.B.: GREAT BRITAIN. This notation is most often seen as an oval bumper sticker identifying automobiles from the British Isles through an internationally agreed system. (see: *U.K.*)

gen: NEWS. 'What's the gen Sam?' 'The bloody government is going to devalue again, that's what.' (see: *bloody*)

gentleman's residence: You will often see this description in the real estate section of New Zealand newspapers. The gentlemen referred to were of the Victorian era and favored two-storied houses, preferably of brick or stone, with high ceilinged rooms and quarters for at least one maid. (see: *villa, property, section*)

(to) get down on: does not mean 'to go down on', although there are similarities. 'I'm getting down on that tin of biscuits at the rate of knots.' 'I'm EATING that jar of cookies very quickly.' (see: *tin, biscuits, rate of knots*)

get in behind: An instruction to working dogs that has become a national in-group joke. In general usage it says, in a humorous way, 'KEEP YOUR (SUBORDINATE) PLACE' (see: *dogs*)

*get one away — get it away: become 'the beast with two backs'. (see: *have it off, shag, stuff, root, on with, (a) naughty*)

get stuck into: 'Get stuck into this roast' or 'get stuck into that job'. Used in the sense of 'BEGIN VIGOROUSLY'.

get the strap: An extract from Bylaw 32 of the National Bylaws of Education Boards (public schools only) follows:

'(a) . . . head teacher . . . responsible . . . may delegate . . .'

(b) Corporal punishment shall not be inflicted for minor misdemeanours, failure to achieve a desired standard of work or degree of correctness, or for inability to learn or neglect to prepare home lessons. If inflicted at all, it is to be reserved for serious offences and administered only if likely to act as a deterrent to further misconduct. In no case is it to be needlessly severe, and it is never to be inflicted except after due consideration.

(c) Corporal punishment, when used shall be inflicted with a natural leather strap (undivided) not exceeding 18 in. in length and not less than

$1\frac{1}{2}$ inches in width and on the palm of the hand. Punishment with any other instrument, or with the hand, or on any other part of the body is expressly forbidden.

(d) Only in exceptional circumstances should girls be strapped and in no case is corporal punishment to be inflicted on girls over 10 years of age.

(e) Records . . . shall be kept . . .

(f) . . . secondary pupils . . . may . . . within the spirit of this Bylaw . . . inflict . . . by means other than that specified in sub-clause (c).' (see: *cane*)

get the wind up — windy: I get the wind up when faced with a deadline. Most drivers who have been drinking get windy when they see that flashing red light. Anxious, worried, or AFRAID.

get your knickers in a twist: is to GET UPSET, as indeed you would be if the underwear you were wearing got all knotted up. 'Calm down, Sam, don't get your knickers in a twist, we'll get it all sorted out.'

gidday: 'Gidday mate,' a traditional greeting. Now heard more often in the country than the city, it means 'GOOD DAY friend'. (see: *eryaguan, owsidgawn*)

gig lamps: Originally used to refer to the two headlight-like lamps used at night to illuminate the road before a horse and carriage. The similarity in appearance has, as gigs get scarcer, shifted the meaning of this term to refer to the GLASSES you wear (I wear) on the end of your (my) nose. From a slightly later era of transportation comes another term for these glasses, i.e. goggles.

gink: (North Island) 'Have a gink at that.' LOOK at that.

girdle: (A) The well known foundation (?) garment.

(B) The GRIDDLE of your stove. (see: *false friends*)

Girl Guides: The local version of GIRL SCOUTS right down to the cookies.

give blood: One gives it for free and gets it (when needed) for free in New Zealand. Such a system only works when a substantial portion of the community is willing to support it. This used to be called 'doing one's civic duty'. The fact that it works in New Zealand is a most favorable comment on the country.

give us a hand: It's the royal me. 'Give us a hand' is 'GIVE ME A HAND', and more likely to be a polite order, than a request.

gizago: 'If you can't solve that problem gizago.' Give us a go, meaning LET ME TRY. (see: *fair go*)

glad rags: a very commonly used term for PARTY CLOTHES.

glasshouse: If your tour guide says he is going to show you a glass house, it's not Hester's residence, but a GREENHOUSE.

Gleneagles agreement: Prior to the 1977 meeting of the Commonwealth heads of government meeting in London, representatives of five of these states got together in an hotel (called Gleneagles) in Scotland to work out a formula that would allow N.Z. to participate in Commonwealth sporting activities (particularly the 1978 Commonwealth Games in Canada) without objection from her sister states (see: *All Blacks*). The ostensible purpose of this meeting was to work out a 'Commonwealth Statement on Apartheid in Sport', however, as N.Z. was the only country under fire from the other Commonwealth nations for sporting contact with South Africa the compromise was pointed at N.Z.

The representatives at Gleneagles were Trudeau (Canada), Manley (Jamaica), Yar Adua (Nigeria), Jumbe (Tanzania) and (see:) *Muldoon*, (New Zealand). Paragraphs 3 and 4 (of 6) of the statement read as follows:

'Mindful of these and other considerations, they accepted it as the urgent duty of each of their governments vigorously to combat the evil of *apartheid* by withholding any form of support for, and by taking every practical step to discourage, contact or competition by their nationals with sporting organizations, teams or sportsmen from South Africa or from any other country where sports are organized on the basis of race, colour or ethnic origin.

'They fully acknowledged that it was for each government to determine in accordance with its laws the methods by which it might best discharge these commitments. But they recognized that the effective fulfilment of their commitments was essential to the harmonious development of Commonwealth sport hereafter.' (Keesings Contemporary Archives Aug 12, 1977. p. 28507).

Unfortunately, like everything else such a formulation is subject to interpretation. The opponents of South Africa have put the emphasis on paragraph 3. The Muldoon Government (with the notable exception of the Deputy Prime Minister) has put the emphasis on the 1st part of paragraph 4 and has assumed that it is enough to say to N.Z. sporting bodies something like the following —

'If you wish to consult us about sending teams to South Africa we will tell you it isn't a good idea, however, this is a free country and you needn't consult us, nor as a free country are we about to refuse passports to citizens who wish to travel for whatever purpose.'

This interpretation has not proved popular with the African members of the Commonwealth. This being my own forum I'll put my 2 cents worth in. I'm in favor of sporting contacts with South Africa under the following conditions: Teams which go to South Africa should be racially mixed and chosen by merit and they should only play teams chosen the same way with the same racially mixed composition! In my opinion change will not come about from total refusal to deal with South Africa but rather a combination of the carrot and the stick. 'We will play if you meet our terms,' rather than 'we won't play until you change your whole society'. Evolution not revolution is, in my arrogant opinion, the way to go.

globe: That's the thing that lights up when you flip the switch. A LIGHT BULB usually has a bayonet base rather than the Edison screw base you are used to, but don't worry if you are bringing screw type lamps over, the bulbs are now available from specialty lamp shops. (see: *switches, hot points, false friends*)

glory box: Did you ladies have a HOPE CHEST as a girl? (see: *bottom drawer*)

gnashers: Gnashers are what you use to chew your food (TEETH). (see: *choppers*)

goals: It is commonly stated that: 'A Kiwi's aim in life is two cars, a bach, and a boat.' Vast quantities of beer are taken for granted. (see: *bach*)

go bush: Someone who leaves his usual haunts, friends and possibly family, most often precipitously, has gone bush. The civilian version of AWOL. The Australian equivalent is to go walkabout.

go for a burn: TAKE A SPIN in a motor vehicle.

go (going) like the clappers: To proceed with speed or to GO LIKE HELL.

(to) go rude at: To exercise the fine art of the INSULT with respect to someone.

Godzone: This is Godzone country and don't let nobody tell you different (God's own). The foregoing being understood Godzone is often used as a synonym for NEW ZEALAND. 'How long have you been in Godzone?'

(it) goes like a bomb: Usually refers to a car, but any mechanical device can 'go like a bomb'. Strangely enough this means that it is GOING WELL. (see: *go like the clappers*)

goggle box: Sometimes without the g. Idiot box or TELEVISION SET to you. You will see some familiar faces. Maude strides across the screen, and Sonny and Cher (yes; and some of the shows are that old) also strut their stuff. (see: *telly*)

Golden Kiwi: New Zealand's NATIONAL LOTTERY. Proceeds go to research and good works. Tickets are a bargain at $1 unless you need the $1. You have one chance in 77 to win something (minimum $10, maximum $60,000). It also has a big brother called the Golden Kiwi 5 + 5. Tickets cost $10 and you can win from $50 to $500,000 (one chance in 50 of winning something). (see: *Tatts, Bonus Bonds, T.A.B.*)

Golden Shears: New Zealand's championship sheep shearing contest. Held in Masterton (north-east of Wellington) each year, it is a very major event for the whole country. Points are awarded, not only for speed, but also for a clean job; nicking the hide is not allowed. The participants show incredible skill, shearing about 20 sheep in an hour. If you read *The Mayor of Casterbridge*, you will find that in Hardy's day, it took the same time to do two sheep. (see: *sheep, primary products*)

Golden Syrup: a brand name SUGAR SYRUP ubiquitous in Kiwi kitchens. It is like maple syrup without the maple. Used for baking and general sweetening. A less common, but just as traditional use for Golden Syrup is at stag parties where the prospective bridegroom is first covered with a layer of shoe polish (*Nugget* is preferred), then a layer of Golden Syrup is applied and this is liberally sprinkled with dots of a multicolored, hard sugar, cake decoration called 'hundreds and thousands'. (see: *hundreds and thousands*)

good on yer — good on you: a term of approbation. Means, roughly, GOOD FOR YOU.

goosegogs: a slang term for CHINESE GOOSEBERRIES or KIWI FRUIT. A major export item and delicious. This term also refers to the original gooseberry, a grape-sized fruit. (see: *Chinese gooseberries, Kiwi fruit*)

gorse: those bushes by the roadside covered with pretty yellow flowers are the farmer's bane. Originally imported from Scotland for use (here as there) as hedges and fences, these thorny bushes adapted to New Zealand's climate with a vengeance. Each winter in its native clime, the gorse freezes and this inhibits its spread. In the milder New Zealand winters, the gorse hardly slows down and much of the effort of low country farmers and vacant lot owners is directed at removing this 'noxious weed', often under considerable pressure from local government. Removal isn't easy. Gorse is very hardy. If you burn it, the roots regenerate the plants. Defoliants work, but only if they are strong enough to kill everything else too, and poison the soil for a time. Digging up the roots does work, but it is expensive. Enjoy the pretty yellow flowers.

got tickets on: 'I've got tickets on that bird (car, job. etc.) Means, I've GOT MY EYE ON (I desire) that . . . (see: *fancy*)

Governor-General: Every British Commonwealth country has a direct representative of the British monarch who acts as TITULAR (meaning all show and little power) HEAD OF STATE in Her Majesty's absence. This office is a descendant of the position of Viceroy, (Vice meaning in lieu of and roy meaning royalty). He opens and closes Parliament, gives speeches written by the Government in power and opens new buildings. In other words, he takes on many of the ceremonial duties performed by the U.S. President while leaving the administrative and legislative ones (the real power) to his (see:) *Prime (first) Minister.*

   The Australian Governor-General recently actually exercised one of his putative powers (dissolving Parliament) and raised such a hue and cry that if his party ever gets back into power they will either abolish the office or strip it of any remaining shreds of power.

G.P.O.: GENERAL POST OFFICE. The central post office of any town. It is also the point from which mileages between communities are calculated on N.Z. Automobile Association maps. (see: *Post Office, postie, post*)

grass grub, or **porina:** in a largely pastoral economy, anything that destroys pasture is (a) important and (b) very undesirable. Grass grubs are INSECT LARVAE which can and do leave 50c sized bare spots all over a field, making it resemble a mouldy swiss cheese. A constant battle is waged against these beasties. The latest weapon in this battle is the use of the female sex attractant (pheremone) to persuade all the adult males to mate with thousands of polystyrene beads scattered around. This not only wears them out, but makes it virtually impossible to find a female with whom to mate.

greaseproof paper: WAXED PAPER

greasies: a derogatory name for breaded and deep-fried FISH AND FRENCH FRIES. Let me assure you they are rarely greasy and often delicious. (see: *fish and chips, shark and tatties, chips*)

green fingers: It may be adequate in North America for a home gardener to have a GREEN THUMB but in New Zealand, it is green fingers that make the garden bloom.

greengrocer: another name for the FRUIT AND VEGETABLE VENDOR (see: *fruiterer*)

greenstone: NEPHRITE JADE native to New Zealand and favored by the Maori for making ornaments (see: *tiki*) and various kinds of warclubs. You can still find large chunks of this in the mountain and glacier country, if you are lucky, and a boulder located by some trampers recently made them all richer by several years' pay. (see: *tramping*)

gridiron: A bunch of big men get dressed up in all kinds of funny protective clothing, divide into two groups and fight over a piece of inflated pigskin. When their frustration level gets really high they kick it amazing distances. In case the description doesn't ring any bells, this is the New Zealand name for the AMERICAN version of FOOTBALL. (see: *football, All Blacks*)

grill: one does not BROIL anything in New Zealand; one grills it instead. In consequence, you can't buy a 'broiler chicken', the closest thing would be a 'roaster'. If you think you have been offered a 'broiler', make sure they didn't say 'boiler'. A menu may well have a section that says 'Grills' referring to steaks and chops cooked over or under an open flame.

grizzle: GRIPE, complain, bellyache, etc. Also 'grizzle guts', a nickname applied to a chronic bellyacher. (see: *winge*)

*grot: (not for use in polite company.) (see: *TOILET, toilet paper, lav., loo, bog, dunny*)

*grunds: MALE UNDERWEAR, independent of its state of cleanliness.

guard's van: That funny little red car at the rear of the train. No one here has ever heard of a CABOOSE.

gum digger: many years ago, a major industry, particularly in the Coromandel Peninsula was digging up the solidified sap of the Kauri tree. This 'Kauri gum' was exported for use in the manufacture of linoleum, paints, etc. Occasionally, unusually beautiful lumps of this transparent golden gum were kept as ornaments, particularly those with insects embedded in them (as in amber). In this degenerate age, the men who dug for Kauri gum have long gone, but their name lives on largely as an adolescent's familiar and somewhat derogatory reference to the family DENTIST. (see: *B.D.S., gumboots*)

gumboots or **gummies:** calf high RUBBER BOOTS characteristically worn by farmers. Don't let that fool you, however, nearly everyone in the country down to the five-year-olds has a pair stashed away somewhere for muddy and/or rainy conditions. I'm told these originated as protective footgear for the men who dug Kauri gum; hence gumboots. (see: *gum diggers, Wellingtons, Southland slippers*)

guts: the commonest use of this term would be in a phrase like 'he's a guts'. This means HE STUFFS HIMSELF WITH FOOD, or in other words, 'he is always gutsing himself'. We have a more general counterpart slang term in 'greedy guts'. (see: *false friends, what the guts is*)

gym boots: (North Island) or *gym shoes* (South Island); the New Zealand name for BASKETBALL SHOES (see: *sand shoes*)

H

haberdashery: The NOTIONS DEPARTMENT of your local department store. 'Buttons and bows' plus a few things Bob Hope didn't mention, like needles, thread, etc. (see: *manchester, cotton*)

hacked off: 'I'm so hacked off with this job that I'm ready to blow it and piss off to the West Coast.' I'm SO MAD AT (ANGRY WITH) . . . (see: *blow it, piss off, slack me off, West Coast*)

haere mai: The warm and cheerful Maori WELCOME.

hair grips or hair clips: BOBBY PINS. You have to admit the Kiwis are more logical than we are on this one. (see: *clothesgrips, or clothespegs*)

hairdressers: There are no barbers in New Zealand, only hairdressers. Some cater to men and some to women (not many unisex shops outside Auckland/Wellington as yet). You are likely to get a surprise when you go to the men's hairdressers. You are most likely to find the kind of BARBERSHOP you remember from your youth (or do you go back to the days of 4-part harmony?)

When I first came to New Zealand in 1970, the cost of a haircut was 50c. Now I'm afraid the range is around $1.50 to $5.00, as Kiwi barbers try to cope with the fall-off in business brought about by long hair and infrequent haircuts.

haka: CEREMONIAL DANCE OF THE MAORI. The traditional way to express feelings. There is a haka for birth, one for marriage and for death. A haka for happiness, for sorrow, for victory and for defeat. Not to mention damn near anything else —

half cut: What you are after half a bottle of brandy. More than half DRUNK. (See: *pissed, skinful*)

half g: Now superceded by its metric equivalent (2.25 liters). This is the standard sized bottle for taking home draught beer from the hotel. If there are only one or two of you, then 2-3 of these would be standard. Oh, yes, a half g is HALF AN IMPERIAL GALLON bottle, almost always containing draught beer. (see: *flagon, hotel, bottle store, beer, pissed*)

half pie: SORT OF. 'Well, he half pie asked me to marry him.'

hamburgers: A cow of a different color. I can't tell you why they are different (excepting the ubiquitous beetroot) but they are. (see: *hot dogs, bread rolls, beetroot, mince*)

hand brake: Another automobile word that's different. The EMERGENCY BRAKE that you use for parking a lot more often than you use it for emergencies. (see: *bonnet, boot, accelerator, windscreen, mudguard*)

(a) handle of beer: Beer (or other beverage) served in a pint or half pint glass that has a MUG style handle. (see: *beer, jug*)

hangi: A MAORI BARBECUE, except that the food isn't barbecued. The day before your hangi, you must dig a pit 4-6 feet deep. Then go down to the riverbed (with your expert adviser) and select a dozen or so round cantaloupe sized rocks. These must be of a special variety so that they won't crack with the heat. Store these in the bottom of your pit. Early the next morning, build a roaring fire over the rocks and let them get red hot. Rake out the ashes and build up a cone-shaped wall of dirt around the pit. Put in baskets of pork, chicken, kumara, veges, fish wrapped in leaves, etc. Pour water over the hot rocks and as the steam rises quickly complete the dirt dome over your pit enclosing rocks, food and steam. About 8 hours later open the pit and eat well. You and 30 or 40 friends that is! (see: *kumara, veges, rock melon*)

hard case or hard shot: Not a tough guy in the sense of being a criminal, but rather someone with the courage of his or her convictions. A STRONG CHARACTER with equal emphasis on 'strong' and 'character'.

50

A Kiwi lady, I am proud to call my friend, who dances until 1 p.m., manages several rental properties and always has at least two lawsuits going at the same time, would be described as a hard case or hard shot. Oh, yes, I almost forgot, she admits to having passed her 70th birthday, a 'short' while ago. (see: *bushwhacker, false friends, Kiwi*)

hard grafter: The man you want to hire! Gung-ho all the way — this is the Stakhnovite of New Zealand. A HARD WORKER. Chances are you can't hire him — most of this rare species work for themselves.

hard yakker: HARD WORK. (see: *hard grafter*)

has the makings: 'He has the makings of a good worker.' He SHOWS PROMISE of being (becoming) a good worker.

have a go: If you never have a go, you'll never know if you could have done it. (for IT, read: ride a horse, jump from a plane, marry a millionaire, make a million on your own, write a book. Fill in your own fantasy.) TRY

have a look in: is to HAVE A CHANCE. 'The election was a farce. Bazzer gave such a good speech Sam didn't have a look in.' (see: *Bazzer*)

(you) have him: YOU'VE BEATEN HIM (in some sort of contest). (see: *good on you*)

*have it off: COPULATE. (see: *get one away, shag, stuff, root, on with, (a) naughty*)

have me on: PUT ME ON — an attempt to bamboozle. (see: *don't come the raw prawn with me*)

Hawke's Bay: Named by Captain Cook for the man (Sir Edward Hawke, First Lord of the Admiralty) who gave him his command. A rich farming region, it had a 1976 population of 145,061 people, 9,170,000 sheep and 824,000 cattle. The major metropolitan area consists of the twin cities of Napier and Hastings which, with their satellite towns, had a 1976 population of 100,978 people. An area with beautiful beaches, deserted by the standards of the rest of the world, and other tourist attractions such as Napier's Marineland, small but very well done. (see: *North Island*)

head prefect: New Zealand high schools have an internal discipline system manned by the students themselves. These teenage cops are called prefects and in a semi-military hierarchy, the top student cop is the head prefect. The closest American equivalent would be a CHIEF SCHOOL MONITOR or the gold badge in a school patrol. My wife still fumes about the head prefect at her school who used to hide behind a gate and pop out hoping to catch girls who had their gloves off, i.e. 'out of uniform'. Got your buttons done up, soldier? (see: *school uniform*)

headmaster: A male school PRINCIPAL. This is a position of considerable autocratic authority in New Zealand, very much like being the captain of a ship. (see: *headmistress, masters, head prefect*)

hells bells and buggy wheels: You lose so much when you shorten things. (see: *my eye [and Bessie Martin]*)

hessian: This is very fancy stuff. Screen printed it is used to cover the walls in some of the most elegant homes. Perhaps we would do the same if it had such an elegant name in North America. Unfortunately we call it BURLAP.

hockey: A very popular game (especially for the girls) in New Zealand.

Also, from your point of view, a very false friend. This is not North American Ice Hockey. Instead it is the original (?) game played on an open field. As the original, they can call it just hockey while we are forced to add the adjective. (see: *curling, false friends*)

honey pot/bomb: For those who have travelled in the Far East, this term will conjure up odiferous memories of night soil. Not so in New Zealand. Here it is the name of that swimming pool spectacular, spectator drenching dive, you know as a CANNONBALL dive. (see: *belly buster, duck dive*)

honours: (A) The Queen's Birthday Honours List. The N.Z. government rewards the faithful, the enterprising, the good and the brilliant by nominating them for:

K.B.E. (Knight Commander of the Civil Division of the Most Excellent Order of the British Empire)

Knight Bachelor of the Most Excellent Order of the British Empire (called Sir but doesn't rate any initials.)

O.B.E. (Officer of the Civil Division of the Most Excellent Order of the British Empire; the Beatles got this one. It is also known by the rude or jealous as 'Other Bugger's Efforts'.)

M.B.E. (Member of the Civil Division of the Most Excellent Order of the British Empire)

Most Kiwis who are honored get one of the above. However, there are also Knights and lesser orders of the Garter, of the Thistle, Bath, of the Order of St. Michael and St. George, the Royal Victorian Order, the Order of Companions of Honour etc. etc. etc. (see: *Queen's Birthday, bugger*)

(B) A four year university degree program that requires good grades to enter and extra work plus the extra year (ordinary Bachelor degrees are three years). This degree, if taken with distinction, can allow a student to proceed to a Doctorate without getting a Master's along the way. (see: *Uni, varsity, false friends*)

hoo-ha: When the streaker came by everyone made a great hoo-ha over a little nothing. FUSS. (see: *Patricia Bartlett*)

hooker: A RUGBY term referring to a front row PLAYER whose job it is to hook the ball out of a scrum with his foot and get it to a waiting team mate outside this organized pileup. So don't look shocked when that husky young man you've been talking to in the hotel tells you, with some pride, that he is a hooker. (see: *All Blacks, football, scrum, hotel, false friends*)

hooley: A hooley is a WILD PARTY. This can be a good thing, or a bad one, depending on whether you are a guest or a neighbor.

hoon: TURKEY (human variety). This expression is largely confined to the southernmost part of the South Island. (see: *prawn, drongo, Southland*)

hooray (pronounced hurray): A Canadian lass, new to New Zealand, was mortally offended the other day when, as she was leaving a party, several people said 'hooray'. It was much later that she discovered that in New Zealand, this is a FRIENDLY GOODBYE. (see: *cheery bye, false friends*)

Hoover: Just as the everyday word for all brands of facial tissues in the United States has become *Kleenex*, originally a brand name, so has

Hoover become the everyday name for VACUUM CLEANER in New Zealand; also independent of brand name. (see: *lux, Banda, Biro, Snowtex*)

*Hori: A patronizing name applied to a Maori. (see: *Pakeha, Maori, coconut*)

hostel: That's a university DORMITORY (heaters are on 7-9 a.m. and 6-12 p.m.) and New Zealand winters are cold! Brr!! Also no heat in the loo. (see: *loo, central heating*)

hot dogs: A banger (SAUSAGE) ON A STICK covered with batter, and then dipped in tomato sauce. Not one of your gastronomic delights. (see: *tomato sauce, bangers, hamburgers, bread rolls, false friends*)

hot pies: Sorry to disappoint you, no chance of a piece of hot apple pie. These are SAVORY PIES, meat or mince. (see: *meat pie, mince pie, savouries, steak and kidney pie*)

hot points (or points): ELECTRICAL OUTLETS (220 volt, 50 cycle). Note that each usually has its own switch. Note also that these switches, like light switches, are ON when they point downwards and OFF when they point upwards. Forgetting can be a frustrating experience. (see: *switches*)

hot water cylinder: In most New Zealand homes, the HOT WATER TANK is located in a closet that doubles as a linen cupboard. This warm, dry place is good not only for airing the washing but also for germinating bean sprouts, making yoghurt, etc. An ecologically sound way of using 'waste' heat, considerably older than New Zealand's ecology movement. (see: *air the washing, califont*)

hotel: (A) licensed hotel – a place 'licensed to sell spirituous liquors'. One requirement of the licence is that accommodation be provided (except for a new innovation called a tavern). This accommodation is, in most cases, a very secondary thing; with the profits being made from pumping up beer from the vast vats under the establishment. In country places the rooms are often permanently booked by local bachelors with jobs that are subject to transfer, e.g. the constable. Normal closing time for such establishments is 10 p.m. (weekdays); however, this regulation is often honored in the breach, particularly in more remote districts where the hotel is the sole public gathering place. I have been told of a hotel on the West Coast, where the constable was resident, that followed a strict tradition. At 10 p.m. the innkeeper would (under the uniformed constable's watchful eye) call 'time, gentlemen, please'. Everyone would drink up and leave. Meanwhile, the constable would go upstairs and change into civvies in time to come back down to the BAR and join the rest of the male community. Which had, of course, returned to the bar with the departure of the constable's 'official' presence.

(B) private hotel – provides food and accommodation, often in a homelike atmosphere. Does not sell booze. (see: *beer, booze barn, public bar, lounge bar, six o'clock swill, bottle store, boozer, West Coast*)

hottie: Remember when you were a kid (assuming that was some time ago) and you caught a cold? Your mother used to bundle you into bed with a HOT WATER BOTTLE for company. This tradition has not died out in New Zealand and most homes will boast at least one hottie and a knitted wool bag to put it in while in use. This bag makes it much nicer to cuddle into than the unadorned rubber would be.

house: Means what you think it does, but is also used in place of *building* when that building has a formal name, e.g. New Zealand House is the building which houses the New Zealand Embassy in London. (see: *false friends*)

Housie: The local version of BINGO. The cards are smaller, and usually blackout is the only game played. Many hotels have a Housie night at least once a week, and there are people who travel from game to game playing every night of the week.

hu hu grub: The EDIBLE LARVAL form of a moth found in downed and decaying trees. A Maori delicacy in the days before effete Pakeha ways took hold. They are, of course, traditionally eaten alive. In a quick survey of friends and acquaintances, I was only able to find one who would admit to having eaten (not enjoyed) this tidbit. He had to eat them as part of a 'survival' exercise when serving with the Territorials. (see: *Maori, Pakeha, Territorials*)

humpty: Pull your easychair up by the fire, put your feet up on the OTTOMAN, relax and read that good novel you've been saving for a cold and rainy winter's day like this one. (see: *pouf, scats*)

Hundreds and Thousands: You will, on occasion, be offered frosted cakes or cupcakes with TINY MULTICOLORED BITS OF CANDY scattered like glitter over the surface. These bits of candy are called Hundreds and Thousands. (see: *biscuit, cookie*)

huntaway: A huntaway is a NOISY (barking) WORKING DOG used to drive sheep, cattle or recently, deer to new paddocks. Generally these dogs are used for gross control such as pushing a flock out of one area into another. Strong-eyed dogs are used for fine control. These dogs are one of the major reasons for the success of New Zealand's pastoral economy, as one man and his dogs here tend to easily do the work that three shepherds (with or without dogs) do elsewhere. (see: *strong-eyed bitch, dogs, dog trials*)

I

I'm not fussed about: 'I'm not fussed about Charlie's new house, the rooms are too small and the toilet is in the bathroom.' I DON'T THINK MUCH OF . . . (see: *bathroom, loo, toilet*)

I didn't come down in the last shower: I'M NO GREENHORN.

ice blocks: Usually refers to ICE CUBES (North Island) but the term is also used for POPSICLES (shaped much like a *Good Humor* bar). (see: *quenchers*)

ice cream soda spoon: ICED TEA SPOON. (see: *spider*)

iced buns: This term refers to New Zealand's closest approximation to coffeecake. Sort of a HOT DOG BUN WITH PINK ICING, thinly sprinkled with COCONUT on top. Not a winner. (see: *bread roll*)

icing sugar: When your American recipes call for CONFECTIONER'S SUGAR, use icing sugar. (see: *cinnamon*)

in a tick: 'I'll be with you in a tick.' I'll be with you IN A SECOND or a tick of the clock.

in the hand: 'You want me to talk that sheila into going to the party with us? It's in the hand (EASY). Just watch me.' (see: *sheila, piss in the hand*)

industrial action: The union is out on STRIKE. It has been suggested that New Zealand has the British disease. If so, this is confined to a few unions with clout and militant leaders. The ones you are most likely to hear about are the wharfies, the Northern Drivers Union, the freezing workers and the Wellington Boilermakers Union. (see: (the) *British disease, industrial unrest, wharfies, freezing workers*)

industrial unrest: The union is THREATENING TO STRIKE, or the industry has had a series of strikes and more are anticipated. (see: *F.O.L., industrial action*)

Inland Revenue: INTERNAL REVENUE. They take a rather larger bite in New Zealand than in the United States. However, in some ways you get more for it. For instance, Public Hospitals are free to New Zealand residents and medical bills are substantially subsidized. A breakdown of the (October '78) earned income taxation structure for a person without dependents:

Yearly Taxable Income	% Tax	Actual Tax
$ 5,000	17%	842.50
10,000	27%	2,742.50
15,000	34%	5,142.50
20,000	39%	7,822.50
25,000	43%	10,722.50

(see: *IR 12, P.A.Y.E.*)

Insurance Companies: That sounds perfectly reasonable doesn't it. Then why are they INSURANCE AGENCIES on the other side of the Pacific?

Intermediate: (A) The FRESHMAN year of a University Science degree is called the Intermediate year. If it is an Arts degree the first year is called a prosaic Stage I. (see: *Uni, Varsity*)

(B) JUNIOR HIGH SCHOOL. (see: *school, college*)

IR 12: N.Z. Inland Revenue form 12, the equivalent of a U.S. Internal Revenue form W2. (see: *Inland Revenue*)

J

jam: Boil up your fruit, do not strain out the pulp, add your syrup and cook again. Spreads beautifully on bread (see: *jelly, bilberry, money for jam*)

jandals: Terms which will not be understood are: THONGS, GO-AHEADS, FLIP-FLOPS, ZORIS. These are (primarily) purchased at a New Zealand-wide chain of stores, in addition to shoe stores, called Para Rubber stores, and are all made of rubber.

January: Summer vacation time — all factories shut! Almost all wholesalers shut! Many retailers shut (at least part of the time)! Your boss, your secretary and your cleaning service are on vacation. Relax and enjoy it, the sun is shining and the summertime beaches are inviting. (see: *Christmas, school holidays*)

jelly: 'Ice cream and jelly and a punch in the belly.' The logic of children's rhymes is beyond me. I think you have to grow up in a culture to understand this sort of thing.

    (A) jelly is JELLO.

    (B) jelly is also STRAINED JAM (see: *jam*)

jersey: Any warm SWEATER whether jumper or cardigan. Called jerseys from the isle off the northern coast of Great Britain where the style originated. (see: *jumper, cardigan, twin set and pearls*)

(Hamilton) jet boat: This is one of the best recent examples of Kiwi ingenuity. Parts of New Zealand have a boating problem similar to that of the Florida Everglades. In swift flowing mountain streams, there is often only 4-6 inches of water at spots while other areas are comfortably manageable. In the still waters of the Everglades, this was solved by removing the protruding outboard motors and mounting aircraft type propellers on the tops of flat bottomed barges; a solution clearly impractical for swift flowing mountain streams. So a man named Hamilton, living in the mountains near Mt. Cook (N.Z.'s highest) applied the same principle that propels squid and jet aeroplanes. Water is sucked in toward the front of the engine and squirted forcefully out the back. These boats go upwards of 35 m.p.h. and, at speed, draw no more than 4 inches of water. It is the only kind of boat that has gone through the Grand Canyon going upstream. If you are in Queenstown, take the Shotover River Jet Boat ride. Disney would have grabbed it for Adventureland. (see: *concrete yacht*)

Jnr: One of the banes of my life (see: *loo*) is this abbreviation for junior in New Zealand, as Jr. is in the United States. Furthermore, no one seems to be able to understand why you feel this should be part of your (my) name when Sr. is 10,000 miles away. grrr!!

Joe Bloggs — Joe PakiPaki from Opunaki: Is the non-existent 'ordinary' Kiwi (JOHN DOE).

joker: . . . then this joker comes out and tells me that my credit's no good so I hauls off and pops him one. GUY. (see: *bloke*)

jolly dee: *O.K.* Husband: 'I'm off to visit the Ballaghs.' Wife: 'Jolly dee.' (see: *right oh, righty oh*)

judder bar: When you are driving down the road and come to a point where the powers that be want to ensure that you slow down, whether you wish it or not, you will find asphalt or concrete ridges placed transversely across the road a short distance (up to 30 cm or 12 inches) apart. These SPEED BUMPS make your vehicle, and your teeth, judder.

jug: (A) Remember those vats of beer under the hotels? Well, when it is pumped up to the bar it usually gets hosed into one of these ONE LITER PITCHERS (they used to be 2 imperial pints). (see: *beer, hotel*)

    (B) hot water jug (POT) used to make the vital ingredient for endless cups of tea.

jumble sale: A more descriptive phrase than a WHITE ELEPHANT SALE. These are most often held for the benefit of a church or school. The goods sold are usually donated by parishioners or parents.

jumper: Not an athlete, not a Calveras county champion (frog, to those who haven't read Mark Twain for a while), but a warm woolly knitted PULLOVER or SWEATER. Since Kiwis kept their thermostats at 68°F or lower by choice, long before it became fashionable in the rest of the world, jumpers indoors and out are very popular clothing. (see: *cardigan, central heating, jersey, twin set and pearls*)

junket: Made with milk, and an enzyme called rennet that causes milk to clot, this (thin) yoghurt textured dessert is an acquired taste. If you are a yoghurt fan you might give this a cautious try. With fruit flavorings, or a sprinkling of nutmeg, junket is a favorite of children and the preference lasts into adulthood. (see: *Marmite*)

just like a bought one: HOME BUILT or home repaired and (hopefully) WORKING WELL. (see: *Do you think it would pass in a crowd?*)

K

kack: (A) MUCK
  (B) EXCRETORY PRODUCTS

kack-handed: The not very nice Kiwi way of saying SOUTHPAW. I have heard it suggested that the first word in the phrase has something to do with the use for which the Arabs reserve their left hands. (see: *kack*)

kai: Maori word for FOOD which has come into general use. (see: *Maori, tucker*)

katipo spider: (LATRODECTUS KATIPO) is about an inch across and has a large egg shaped middle with a red stripe down the center. Closely related to the black widow, it is, as far as I know, the only poisonous, land living, member of the animal kingdom in New Zealand. Not a usual beach companion, they do appear in bunches when you find them. Don't play with that nice red striped spider, you may (unlikely) see on a sandy beach anywhere north of Christchurch. (see: *snakes*)

Kauri: When Captain Cook first explored New Zealand in 1769 he wrote an enthusiastic report for the British Navy. This report concerned neither the planting of colonies nor the mineral wealth of New Zealand. What Cook was selling the Navy were these ruler straight, incredibly tall HARDWOOD TREES. Just the thing for the thousands of masts needed by a world girdling sailing ship navy.

Later, the gum (sap) from these trees became a major export item, going into varnishes and linoleum. The wood, especially the heartwood, of the Kauri was especially valued for building and fine furniture. As with any such item in a frontier economy, it eventually became scarce and the trees are now protected pending the centuries-long tasks of regeneration and reforestation. One of the best places to see these today is the Coromandel Peninsula (look east from Auckland on your map). (see: *gumdigger, Auckland (Central)*)

keen: A GOOD KEEN MAN is the title of one of the excellent and hilarious books by Barry Crump. He is New Zealand's ethnic author where Pakehas are concerned. His stories are usually in rural settings of the 1930's and 40's but the flavor remains the same. Keen tends to mean REALLY INTERESTED or SHARP. 'I'm keen to get to that new trout stream.'

57

'He is a good keen man.'

keep your hair on: DON'T GET YOUR BOWELS IN AN UPROAR.

kerb: The CURB between the sidewalk and the street. (see: *footpath*)

kindy: KINDERGARTEN. These are attended by children 3-5 years of age who usually come two half-days per week. The teachers are trained at Teachers' Colleges. (see: *college*) The governing body is the Free Kindergarten Association which has all its ordinary expenses (teachers' salaries, construction, etc.) paid for by the Government's Ministry of Education. (see: *playcentre, schools*)

kitchen tidy: Sounds like a housemaid; refers to the plastic GARBAGE CAN with a foot operated lid found in every kitchen. (see: *rubbish*)

Kiwi: (A) A flightless relatively sightless, nondescript, nocturnal, brown bird that spends most of its time grubbing in the dirt for a living.

(B) The national symbol of NEW ZEALAND. CITIZENS are proud to call themselves Kiwis. Sound strange? Remember the Bald Eagle is a fish eater, known (by its handlers) for its bad breath. It's the spirit that counts.

Kiwi fruit: (see: *Chinese gooseberries*)

*Kiwi grace: (before meals): '2, 4, 6, 8, bog in, don't wait.' Not heard at the most refined tables. Not heard at moderately refined tables. (see: *bog in, bog*)

knees up (mother Brown): A 'knees up' is a PARTY. This comes from a 1950's English song whose first line 'Knees up, knees up, Mother Brown' can be heard when the middle income-middle-aged get middlin' sloshed (in large group settings).

knickers: (A) Oh, this one will take you back; about a generation. Ladies underwear, PANTIES. (see: *sheila, Witches Britches*)

(B) Also used as a swearword by those for whom 'darn' is a bit too strong.

knock up: A sweet little old lady from New Zealand arrived in San Francisco, checked into her hotel room, and just before retiring for the night said to the flabbergasted young man at the front desk, 'Please knock me up at 8 a.m. Good night.' All she was asking for was a MORNING CALL.

knuckle sandwich: What you offer the obviously hungry individual who has stepped on your toe, spilt beer in your lap and implied that you have canine ancestry on your mother's side. A PUNCH IN THE FACE. (see: *dial, to get your face smacked in, a bunch of fives*)

kumara: A SWEET POTATO like root vegetable introduced into New Zealand by the Maoris. Like most other root crops, it looks unattractive in its raw state, but you can prepare it in any way that you would an ordinary potato and it will taste better in 90% of those preparations. (see: *Maori*)

L

Labour Party: No I haven't misspelled it. Lots of words pick up an extra u in New Zealand. Officially called the New Zealand Labour Party to differentiate it from other parties of the same name around the globe. This is the second, and more socialistic, of New Zealand's two major parties. In 1978 the Labour Party was at first thought to have received a plurality of the popular vote (it didn't) but got fewer representatives in Parliament, because of the distribution of that vote (i.e. Labour voters were concentrated in fewer electoral districts). This party has close ties to the F.O.L. (New Zealand's A.F.L.-C.I.O.) but this proved of scant help in dealing with 'industrial unrest' when Labour was in power. (see: *National Party, Values Party, Social Credit Party, Potty Party, Parliament, F.O.L., industrial unrest, industrial action, Words*)

ladies a plate (gents a crate): It's a party (invitation) with the female guests providing the food and, most likely, the male guests providing the drink. (see: *B.Y.O.B.*)

lambing: That SEASON of the year when all good farmers are out helping their ewes to give BIRTH, hopefully to a pair of twin baby LAMBS apiece.

land agent: There are those who would feel that this term is equivalent to road agent; however, he is merely your friendly, hard-working REAL ESTATE AGENT.

larrikin — larrikinism: A larrikin is a WILD YOUNG MAN. Larrikinism is what such a young fellow *might* engage in: VANDALISM. (see: *yahoo, yob-yobbo*)

late night: Between government regulations and union rules shopping hours in New Zealand are severely restricted. It has long been a tradition that people should work a 40 hour week with their weekends free and this applies to (see:) *shop assistants* as well as the rest of the work force. One concession is usually made to the fact that most people are otherwise employed during normal 9-5.30 shop opening hours. This concession is called a late night (SHOPS OPEN 9 A.M. TO 9 P.M.) and each shopping area holds one per week. Friday night is the usual time but in larger centers Thursday and even Wednesday nights are the late nights for peripheral shopping areas who profit from being open when they have no competition from the central shopping district. Operating on the same principle, resort areas, particularly those within reach of a large city, often have their 'late night' on Saturday morning. (see: *shop, dairy*)

laundrette: LAUNDRAMAT.

lav: (see: *TOILET, toilet paper, loo, bog, dunny, grot, bathroom*)

lay-by: Yes, we have it in New Zealand, too. The LAY-AWAY with time to pay at your friendly department store. (see: *hire purchase, on the never never*)

leading hand: Another way of saying FOREMAN. (see: *charge hand*)

Lecturer — Senior Lecturer: Academic rank roughly corresponding to ASSISTANT-ASSOCIATE PROFESSOR in the U.S. (see: *Professor, Reader, Associate Professor, Chair, false friends*)

leg-in: A leg-in section is a HOUSING LOT that is located away from the road and BEHIND ANOTHER HOUSE or houses. These are often the quietest and most pleasant, but they are very hard for first-time guests to find.

leg-up: It used to refer to helping someone mount his horse; 'let me give you a leg up.' Now it refers to HELPING someone GET AHEAD in a job or recreational activity.

legal age for drinking: 20 YEARS. For voting it is 18 years, for sex, it is 16 years. Doesn't reflect your priorities? Why not? Why should it? (see: *age of consent*)

lemonade: If it looks like 7UP or SPRITE and it tastes like *7UP* or *Sprite*, then it is lemonade. What you think of as lemonade is lemon cordial. (see: *cordial, fizzy drink*)

lever: Pronounced (leever), same meaning, different sound.

licensed hotel: A hotel that can legally indulge your taste for a drop of liquid cheer. (see: *hotel, beer, boozer, booze barn*)

lieutenant: Pronounced leftenant — same meaning.

lift: ELEVATOR.

lines: I will not talk in class
        I will not talk in class
        I will not talk in class
        I will not talk in class
        I will not talk in class
        I will not talk in class
        I will not talk in class
        I will not talk in class
        I will not talk in class
        I will not talk in class
        I will not talk in class
        I will not talk in class
            etc.   etc.   etc.

litre: A liter is a metric measure (see: *metrication*) of liquid volume. It is equal to 1.057 U.S. quarts or .88 Imperial quarts (see: *gallon*). Beer and petrol are now, by Government fiat, sold by the liter which confuses everyone including the salespeople. (see: *beer, jug, half g, petrol, Words*)

local rag: The best quality paper has some old rags in its manufacture. This is your HOMETOWN NEWSPAPER. Like the U.S. and unlike the U.K. (United Kingdom = Great Britain), there are no national daily papers, each region and town of any size has its own. Local news takes priority in the small town papers, and plurality in the city papers. (see: *U.K., Sunday papers, Saturday papers*)

lollies: What the kids badger you for. CANDY of any kind.

lolly scramble: Originally an activity engaged in at kids' parties where double handfuls of candy are thrown on the floor and the kids scramble for them. Rather like what happens when someone finally succeeds in busting a piñata.

   The term now has wider application, as describing any kind of undignified attempt by groups of people to 'get theirs'. The playing off of one political candidate against another in terms of pre-election promises has been described as the 'election time lolly scramble'. (see: *lollies*)

loopies: In the resort areas of New Zealand (particularly Central Otago), the residents and transient workers have a name for those of us who only come to sun, ski, climb or boat. I haven't been able to find the origin of this ungenerous appellation for *tourists* and I'm not sure I want to. (see: *Otago*)

long-nosed pliers: NEEDLE NOSED PLIERS. There are a large number of differences in tool names, only a few of which are recorded herein. (see: *bastard, spanner*)

loo: bathroom (Gardez loo). Kiwis can't figure out why we call a room without a bath a bathroom. TOILETS or loos have their own little rooms in most places, and it is quite difficult to sell a house where the toilet is in the bathroom. In some older houses (30-40 years) you may have to go outside to get to a perfectly modern toilet (without heat) while bath and sink occupy the 'bathroom' in the house.

The term 'loo' is used more by women than men and both sexes usually say toilet. 'John' will be understood but not used. The grosser types refer to this convenience as the 'grot'. (see: *toilet, toilet paper, lav, bog, grot, dunny, bathroom, caught short*)

look the dead spit: 'Beaut baby! Looks the dead spit of his dad!' JUST ALIKE. (see: *beaut*)

lorry: This word is rapidly being replaced by TRUCK as American influence spreads, but you will hear it.

lounge: The lounge of your home is most definitely not for lounging. This is your LIVING ROOM, most often treated as a formal parlor for entertaining visiting strangers or other visitors of high status. The real day-to-day living goes on elsewhere in the house.

lounge bar: This used to be, and still is in some places, the 'Ladies and Escorts Bar'. Unlike the public bar, genteel ladies can drink here and unlike the public bar, seats are provided and, of course, a premium is usually charged for these amenities. (see: *public bar, hotel, licenced hotel, six o'clock swill*)

lowboy: A short man? A low character? A juvenile delinquent? A subservient lad? A low CHEST OF DRAWERS without a mirror on top. (see: *tallboy, duchesse*)

lusty wench: Teenage argot for the GIRL NEXT DOOR, attractive, desirable but respectable. (see: *town bike, scrubber*)

lux: (A) TO VACUUM one's carpet

(B) a VACUUM CLEANER. This, like hoover, is a corruption of a brand name. In this case, *Electrolux*, which appears to be the most widely used vacuum cleaner in New Zealand. (see: *Hoover*)

M

mac or **macintosh:** (A) a RAINCOAT or slicker. Very important, especially in the winter. A 'plastic mac' is a plastic raincoat.

(B) a waterproof, plastic or rubber sheet placed between the bottom sheet and the mattress on the beds of those (usually extremely young or extremely old) who have imperfect bladder control.

mai mai: There you are, crouching, cold, wet (?), and expectant in your little hut among the reeds next to your favorite lake. Duck season is about to open and you await the sunrise and the game in your DUCK BLIND.

main centres: In New Zealand there are traditionally four 'main centres', even though some 'provincial centres' have overtaken the smallest of these in size. The 'main centres' are, from north to south (1976 census), AUCKLAND (area pop. 797,802), WELLINGTON (area pop. 349,628), CHRISTCHURCH (area pop. 325,810) and DUNEDIN (area pop. 120,426). (see: *Words*)

mainland: This depends where you hail from. If you're from the North Island, that's where it is. Likewise with the South. Stewart Islanders, however, haven't yet developed such delusions of grandeur.

The story goes that the god Maui sat on the South Island and fished the North Island out of the sea. That should be pretty conclusive, but the North Islanders say that they have the bulk of the population and the $$. The South Islanders say that they have the bulk of the land, minerals and sheep. It all boils down to where you live. I live in Dunedin, so a clear and impartial reading of the evidence makes it clear that the South Island is the mainland. (see: *pig island, North Island, South Island, Stewart Island*)

maize, or **Indian corn:** That's what you think of as CORN. To a Kiwi, it is a very specialized type of grain. (see: *corn*)

manchester: In the industrial revolution, the city of Manchester specialized in the mass production of things made of cloth. As a result, the manchester department of your local New Zealand department store sells the sheets, towels, etc. The DRY GOODS counter. (see: *drapers, mercers*)

manure: Refers to ANY FERTILIZER, not necessarily animal wastes. To manure is to SPREAD FERTILIZER. (see: *aerial topdressing, super, false friends*)

Maori: (pronounced Mawri). NATIVE NEW ZEALANDER. Well, in some ways, no more native than you are. These Polynesians retain records of their first landings in New Zealand and any group with such good memories is no more a native of New Zealand than you are of North America (unless you are an American Indian). They are just about the only non-pale types you will see (see: *coconut*); copper-colored, with curly black hair. Note this well because it is usually the only detectable difference between the PAKEHA (which see) and the Maori. Their speech is identical and so are many of their customs. Here integration works so well it usually isn't even noticed.

p.s. They haven't eaten anyone for 100 years or more.

*Maori holiday: Like other socioeconomically disadvantaged groups, the Maori is the butt of a number of jokes. (How many Irish, Polish, or Black jokes do you know?) A Maori holiday is THE DAY AFTER PAYDAY. Maoris do not, as a group, have the middle class (Protestant) ethic. That is the idea that work is an end in and of itself. This reminds me of a story about a New York executive who was driving through the Appalachians when he spotted an Indian sitting under a tree. He stopped and, after some preliminaries, the following conversation ensued:

(NY) 'Why don't you come to the city and get a job?'

(I) 'What's in it for me?'

(NY) 'Well, once you get to be an executive you can take Wednesday afternoons off to play golf or just sit under a tree.'

(I) 'I see! Anything else?'

(NY) 'You can get from two weeks to a month off each year, with pay, to visit beautiful spots like this one.'

(I) 'That's nice. Anything else?'

(NY) 'When you get to 65 or so you can retire and buy a house in one of those beautiful spots and just relax.'

(I) 'Under a tree like this one?'

(see: *Maori*)

Maoritanga: MAORI CULTURE.

marae: I'm told this used to refer specifically to the open (ceremonial) ground in front of a Maori meetinghouse. In common usage today, it refers not only to this ground but the meeting house itself and any auxiliary space or buildings.

marching girls: One of New Zealand's less comprehensible phenomena. Imagine teams of 10 to 50 pre-pubescent (and early post) little and middle-sized girls, dressed like the baton-twirlers that accompany High School bands, wearing busbies like the guards at Buckingham Palace. Now remove the batons and train them to march and countermarch like a crack military drill team. The country is overrun with their like. Every hamlet has its team, and please note, this is 'voluntary fun'.

Marlborough: The north eastern corner of the South Island. It's major city is Blenheim (1977 estimated pop. 17,250) and the most striking feature is the Marlborough Sounds, a collection of peninsulas and islands that combine relatively untouched forest and beaches with a very comfortable climate. If you have the time, a cruise (probably starting at Picton) in this region is highly recommended. Now for the obligatory statistics (1976 census); people 35,030; sheep 1,529,000; cattle 141,000. (see: *South Island*)

Marmite and ***Vegemite*:** Flavored and fortified Yeast extracts, which are used like butter as A SPREAD on bread. Popular tradition has it that Marmite is flavoured with beef blood and Vegemite is flavoured with some sort of vegetable extract. Careful examination of the labels on these containers in my local dairy suggests that if this is indeed true, then the manufacturers are keeping that portion of their recipes a secret. Why, you might ask, did I look at it in the dairy rather than purchasing it. Friends, this is an acquired taste! From my point of view I have never found anything with a fouler taste! Kiwis, on the other hand, have been known to scour the grocery stores abroad frantically searching for this concoction, and if they fail, they write desperate letters to New Zealand requesting CARE packages of Marmite or Vegemite. I might add that most Kiwis view the idea of a peanut butter and jelly sandwich very much the way I view a Marmite sandwich, but at least I have tried Marmite. (see: *sandwich, dairy*)

marrow: If you see marrow on a menu, it isn't bone marrow, it's SQUASH. (see: *swedes, beetroot*)

masters: short for schoolmasters or TEACHERS. (see: *headmaster, headmistress, school*)

match: a match can indeed be the familiar red-headed flammable object,

63

but, it is more likely to refer to the meeting of two sports teams on the playing field. A GAME. (see: *test*)

mate: 'me mate' is not the lady to whom I am wed, but rather my FRIEND. (see: *cobber*)

mates rates: If you happen to be a plumber, storekeeper, paperhanger, etc. Mates rates is what you charge your friends, considerably DISCOUNTED from what you charge the general public. Ot course, this works both ways; when you need their services you, too, pay mates rates. (see: *mate*)

Maths or **to do Maths:** MATHEMATICS. To do maths is to undertake a course of study in this subject.

matron: This term always conjures up, for me, a vision of a stout, dignified, married lady of middle years. Wrong again! This is the title of the SUPERVISING NURSE (if female) at a hospital. The ones I am privileged to know tend to be lean, energetic, and of indeterminate age. (see: *sister, false friends*)

M.B., Ch.B.: Bachelor of Medicine and Surgery. This is the degree held by your local family DOCTOR. Note he does not have a doctorate. M.D.'s either come from overseas or if local, have earned the M.D. as a higher (research) degree in medicine. M.B.Ch.B. is a six-year degree. The first year of this is an undergraduate university year and the rest, medical school training. (see: *B.D.S.*)

me: 'me house', 'me car', 'me wife', 'me property'. MY house, etc. A recent fad among middle class men in their 20's and 30's who appear to think they are proclaiming unity with the manual workers. The latter do not, to the best of my knowledge, speak this way.

mean: A mean man could be a very pleasant chap. He does, however, have one failing or virtue, if you are inclined that way, he is MISERLY. (see: *false friends*)

meat and two veg: The STANDARD Kiwi MEAL; consisting of a generous serving of meat and two kinds of vegetable.

meat pie: A (3-4 in. diameter) pastry shell filled with chunks of meat and vegetables. These can be very good, however, a close relation that looks very much the same (mince pie) does not receive the same endorsement. (see: *mince pie, dressed pie, pea, pie and pud; pie cart, savouries*)

mercers — mercery: An establishment which purveys men's clothing to the general public for considerations of a pecuniary nature. A MENSWEAR STORE. This term has lost popularity in recent years, but is still used in provincial centers. (see: *drapers*)

messages: 'I have to go do my messages.' 'Have you done your messages?' Sounds very strange until you learn that messages are ERRANDS.

metal: isn't metallic at all. Metal just means GRAVEL. Usually it means the gravel under the wheels of your car. Roads come in Grades I, II, Metal and Dirt. I and II are sealed. (see: *seal, pavement*)

metrication: the process of shifting from measuring in imperial units (feet, inches, gallons etc.) to metric units (meters, centimeters, liters, etc.) New Zealand built up to this slowly, but when M day came it was drastic. In timberyards, the foremen went around all of the men, took away their folding rulers (marked in inches and sometimes also meters) and replaced them with metric rulers. The day after, I had occasion to go into a timberyard looking for a 6 ft by 4 ft sheet of plywood. All I got was a helpless shrug from the yardman and a request for the metric dimensions as he had no way of converting my requirements.

metric measure	U.S. measure
kilometre	.62 miles
metre	1 yard, 3.37 inches
centimetre	.39 inches
millimetre	.04 inches
hectare	2.47 acres
litre	1.057 quarts
millilitre	.27 fluid ounces
metric ton	2,205.07 lbs
kilogramme	2.205 lbs.
gramme	.035 ounces

U.S. measure	metric measure
mile	1.610 kilometres
yard	.914 metres
foot	30.480 cm
inch	2.540 cm
acre	.405 hectare
gallon	3.785 litres
quart	.946 litres
pint	.473 litres
pound	453.000 grammes
ounce	28.350 grammes

Note that the U.S. liquid measures above do not correspond to the Imperial measurements that go by the same names. If a Kiwi talks about pints, quarts or gallons, he is talking about Imperial measures. (see: *gallon, decimalization, Words*)

mighty: 'How was your trip?' 'Mighty!' How was your trip? TERRIFIC (marvelous)! (see: *boomer, false friends*)

milk: Always pasteurized, rarely homogenized (see: *top of the milk*), and purveyed in real glass 600 ml bottles (1.27 U.S. pints), at 18c a bottle, by a real milkman. Homogenized milk is available; it's just that no-one wants to buy it except for milk-bars where it is used to make milk shakes. Milk, or sometimes top of the milk, is what is customarily put into coffee and tea in place of the North American's customary cream (or in these fat conscious days 'half and half'). I'm told that you should always pour the milk into the tea rather than the tea into the milk, to avoid scalding. However, I'm also told that if you make this error, you are in good company, as the Queen also does this. (see: *top of the milk, litre, Queen, tea, milk-bar*)

milk-bar: The local ICE CREAM PARLOR usually combined with the corner dairy. (see: *dairy, milk-bar cowboy, brown derby, milk*)

milk-bar cowboy: The teenager polishing his macho image at the local ice cream parlor since he's too young to go to the hotel. (see: *legal age for drinking, hotel*)

milk shed: the place where one of New Zealand's foremost primary products passes from bovine to man. These are sophisticated, shiny clean, modern structures designed to elicit maximal co-operation from the cows and allow one or two people to milk massive numbers without help. The actual milking is done with suction cups that feed into hoses and from there to a central reservoir. A smooth, efficient and profitable operation. (see: *milk treatment station*)

milk tokens: New Zealand has retained that distant memory of North American childhood, the milkman. He does, however, drive a truck rather than having the familiar well-trained horse. In some places, there is a problem, in that placing money in milk bottles on your front doorstep isn't always safe. It has occasionally been known to disappear. Consequently each milkman coins his own PLASTIC MONEY; good only for buying milk from him. You purchase this money from your local corner dairy (see: *dairy*) and put it in the milk and cream bottles. (see: *milk*)

milk treatment station: The milk comes from the milk shed on individual farms and is then collected by truck and taken to a (usually co-operatively owned) MILK PROCESSING PLANT where it is pasteurized, and in large part made into butter, cheese and milk powder for export. (see: *milk shed, milk*)

mince: (mincemeat). No one will threaten (in so many words) to make this out of you. Nevertheless, you better ask for steak mince if you want HAMBURGER MEAT (ground beef). Otherwise you will not be understood. Hamburgers per se retain the name but unfortunately the addition of beets, as garnish, and ground mutton doesn't enhance their flavor. (see: *mince pies, hamburgers*)

mince pie: A soupy concoction of mince (hamburger) inside a slightly leathery wheaten crust, usually about 3 inches in diameter. Not recommended. Only around Christmas is this term likely to mean what you think it does. (see: *mince, steak and kidney pie, savouries, hot pies*)

**minge: from fringe perhaps? This term refers to the short and curly pelt which is found in the pelvic triangle of homo sapiens. This particular term usually refers to the female of the species. (see: *short and curlies, privates, crutch — crutching*)

mingy: A cross between MISERLY and dingy — it refers not only to people but to objects. For instance 'that's a pretty mingy piece of pie she sold you'. That's a pretty small and tattered piece of pie she sold you.

mini: mini as in skirt, alas seems to be a past fad (they were so much shorter in New Zealand than in the States at the height of the fad that I had trouble adjusting to the idea that this was a cultural norm rather than a series of aberrant individuals). However, a Mini is a CAR manufactured by *Austin* of England. It is comparatively inexpensive, easy to repair and while small, appears larger on the inside than it is outside. A thoroughly good idea. (see: *Yank tank*)

mini-tanker: a 100 (Imperial) GALLON CONTAINER OF BEER these can be rented for your private parties. (see *gallon, beer, 4 and a half*)

Minister of Finance: is the SECRETARY OF THE TREASURY except that he must be an elected Member of Parliament before he is eligible for appointment to this post. The current Minister appointed himself. He was able to do this because he is also the Prime Minister, and is Chairman of the Governing Board of the International Monetary Fund. (see: *Piggy, Muldoon, Prime Minister*)

Ministers: These come in two varieties, both noted for their loquacious habits, ministers of religion and ministers of the Crown. The latter group are MEMBERS OF THE CABINET and include their leader, the Prime Minister. Who, you might ask, is 'the Crown'? This is the Queen of New Zealand, as represented by Her Governor-General. (see: *Queen, Governor-General, Prime Minister*)

Ministry of Works lure: Warning: devoted fishermen, especially fly fishermen, should not read this item without medical help standing by with massive doses of tranquilizer! First, you set up your net downstream, blocking most of the channel and then you take your M.O.W. lure (a stick of DYNAMITE) and throw it in upstream. The dead and stunned trout accumulate in the net. Not sporting, what? (see: *M.O.W., nickel spinner*)

misunderstanding: This is the general euphemism for PERSONALITY CLASHES. If you come into a place in a trouble-shooting capacity and are told that Mr X and Mrs Y have a misunderstanding about issue Z, this does not mean that a clear explanation of the other side will clear up the misunderstanding. Instead it tends to mean that they understand each other perfectly well and have a fundamental disagreement, or that they just can't stand the sight of each other.

money for jam: Once all your expenses and reasonable needs are covered, any cash left over is money for jam, GRAVY, icing on the cake. In the hard world of England's industrial revolution, bread was the necessary 'staff of life'. Jam on your bread was pure luxury.

M.O.T.: MINISTRY OF TRANSPORT. In New Zealand, the Police and the Traffic Officers are two completely different non-interchangeable organizations. Traffic officers are empowered, only, to deal with motoring offences. The police take care of crimes. Cars (usually black with a white stripe around the middle and marked M.O.T.) with red lights on top, give tickets. Unless you are driving recklessly the (white) ones with two blue lights on top, aren't interested (Police). (see: *pointsman*)

mother, king and country: MOTHER, FLAG, and APPLE PIE.

motorbike: is what a bikie rides. A MOTORCYCLE. The local price of these will set you back on your heels. Trail bikes are working vehicles on nearly every farm, having turned out to be cheaper, faster and much less trouble than dobbin. (see: *bike, push bike, bikie*)

motorcamps: KOA would love these. A place to pitch your tent, park your trailer, and often a very, very simple cabin in which to spread your sleeping-bag, i.e. CAMPGROUND. Most of these are operated by local municipalities. They are cheap, clean and simple. Not for those who want the Hilton, but a marvelous way to meet Kiwis. One word of warning, don't try to stay in one during school holidays unless your nerves are much better than mine. (see: *school holidays*)

motorway: FREEWAY, autobahn, autostrada, etc. Two or more lanes of limited access divided highway. There are short stretches of this near 4 or 5 major centers. The word, however, is unique; your synonyms will usually not be understood.

M.O.W.: THE MINISTRY OF WORKS AND DEVELOPMENT or the GOVERNMENT CONSTRUCTION DEPARTMENT builds dams, roads, buildings, etc. etc. The 'works' are public works and M.O.W. has an army of engineers, draftsmen and laborers who move around the country in an endless round of build and repair. (see: *Ministry of Works lure*)

M.P.: Not a military policeman, but a MEMBER OF PARLIAMENT. (see: *Boys on the Hill, P.M.*)

mountain oyster: Unlike the beautiful Bluff oysters, these do not come in shells. They are the GONADS of RAMS.

muck around or **muck about:** 'He's been mucking about with that car for two months now and he still hasn't gotten it running'. FOOLING AROUND (see: *fart arsing about, puddle around*)

muck in: DIG IN and get the job done. (see: *buck in*)

mudguard: This device is found on your motorcar in the location that might reasonably be expected to house a FENDER. (see: *accelerator, bonnet, boot, hand brake*)

mug: sucker

Muldoon, Robert D.: PRIME MINISTER and Minister of Finance OF NEW ZEALAND. The controversial, blunt spoken leader of the more conservative of New Zealand's two major political parties (the National Party). A spokesman for (closely regulated, and often subsidized) private industry in what is, in many ways, a highly socialist country. (see: *Piggy, P.M., Prime Minister, Noodlum, boys on the hill, Minister of Finance*)

mum or **mummy:** MOM

murder house: At most large schools, and for each collection of small ones, there is a small prefabricated building set slightly apart in which you can find one or more School Dental Nurses who do all of the preventive, and most of the corrective dental work (free) for the children in their schools. Complex problems are referred to a dentist, whose fees are paid by the Department of Education. The children, unlike you and I?, consider a visit to the SCHOOL DENTAL CLINIC an unpleasant necessity, at best. Hence the name. (see: *B.D.S.*)

muster: (A) Roll out the chuckwagon boys, it's ROUND-UP time. Usually (but not always), it is sheep that are being rounded up. (see: *runholder, station, high country station, sheep, primary products*)

(B) A gathering of soldiers. (see: *up to muster*)

mutton dressed up like lamb: an old hen (or rooster) bedecked in the feathers of a spring chicken.

muttonbird: The SOOTY SHEARWATER or puffinus grisens is a petrel (type of seagull). The name muttonbird presumably derives from a similarity in taste between muttonbirds and old sheep (see: *mutton*) I must admit to having chickened out, so far, on this one. The majority of my muttonbird eating friends claim it is greasy and ghastly, a minority claim it is delicious. There seems to be no middle ground. It is the chicks, harvested just before they can fly, that are taken for food and oil. In fact, the copious oil from these birds was once the staple lamp fuel in the South Pacific.

my eye (and Bessie Martin): An expression most often heard in Southland, it means fat chance, or MY FOOT, or I don't believe a word you say. Outside of Southland, my only encounter with this phrase was on a television historical adventure program, called *The Onedin Line*.

N

N.A.F.T.A.: New Zealand-Australia, Free Trade Agreement. This appears to be an agreement on how to limit free trade. Australia sells N.Z. twice as much as it buys in dollar values, but everytime N.Z. manufacturers succeed in opening up an Australian market a mighty protectionist howl goes up on the other side of the Tasman, and the N.Z. manufacturer has to look for new overseas markets, or just gives up and goes back to supplying the domestic markets. N.Z. too limits manufactured imports from Australia (particularly automobiles) rigidly, which gives the Aussies a peg on which to hang their complaints. (see: *white goods, trans-Tasman, Aussie*)

nanna: Pronounced like banana, it means GRANDMOTHER. This is babytalk that lasts into maturity.

nappies or napkins: This is always good for a laugh — usually at me. One simply does not go around asking for a DIAPER in the best restaurants. A napkin is a diaper. A serviette is what you must ask for when you want a napkin.

(to) nark: to irritate or nag or to RIDE. 'If you don't quit narking me about that $5 I'll stuff it down your throat'. (see: *take the mickey*)

National Party: The less socialistic of N.Z.'s two (socialist) major parties. This party is thought of, by Kiwis, as the equivalent of the Republican Party in the U.S. As far as economic policy goes it is actually considerably to the left of the left wing of the Democratic Party. On the other hand, its non-economic policies are right wing somewhere between the center and Senator Goldwater. The National Party has achieved that degree of electoral superiority that the Democrats seem to have in the U.S. In other words they have run the country with the exception of 3 years out of the last 19 (as of 1979) and 23 of 34 years since the second World War. In 1978 the party scraped up a plurality (barely, at first it was thought they hadn't) of popular votes but a comfortable majority of Parliamentary seats. (see: *Labour Party, Values Party, Social Credit Party*)

national programme: The YA radio stations that carry news, commentary, drama, and music (at the level of show tunes). A subsidiary of B.C.N.Z. (see: *B.C.N.Z., concert programme, wireless*)

natter: 'Let's have a natter about that'. Let's have a TALK about that.

(a) naughty: To have CARNAL KNOWLEDGE of a member of the opposite sex. My, how the terminology doth change, while the behavior remains relatively constant. (see: *shag, have it off, get one away, root, on with, false friends, bit of crumpet*)

neateh: neat, eh? AIN'T IT THE BERRIES? or, GOOD ISN'T IT?

neither use nor ornament: Evocative isn't it? I'd hate to be described this way.

Nelson: This region consists of the north western corner of the South Island. Its major city is also called Nelson and has a metropolitan population of 42,433 (1976). An area of mild climate, beautiful beaches, apple orchards and the inevitable 859,000 sheep, 164,000 cattle and 75,562 people to look after their welfare. (see: *South Island)*

netball: A version of OUTDOOR BASKETBALL played mostly by girls. Seven to a side, no dribbling, no backboard.

nett: net, as in profit. (see: *gaol, programme, Words*)

New Zealand Christmas tree: A beautiful green tree with lovely red flowers that bloom in the middle of summer, i.e. at Christmas time. Its other name is the POHUTAKAWA. (see: *seasons*)

nickel spinner: Another horror story for the devoted fisherman. A BULLET (not necessarily nickel plated) fired at a trout (or any other fish). This almost always misses but it stuns the fish which then float to the surface to be gathered in. (see: *Ministry of Works lure*)

nifty: CLEVER or EFFICIENT or WELL DESIGNED. 'Mavis had a nifty idea which she executed in a nifty fashion, something you wouldn't expect from such a nifty looking bird.'

nightdress: NIGHTGOWN (see: *nightie*)

nightie: Those frilly NIGHTDRESSES worn by the fair sex and by some members of the unfair sex. (see: *nightdress*)

9 o'clock flu: A disease that strikes workers and schoolchildren only during weekdays. Weekends are miraculously free of this disorder. (see: *take a sickie*)

Nippon-clipon: The AUCKLAND HARBOR BRIDGE was once a two-lane bridge (one in each direction). Thanks to New Zealand money and Japanese engineering, it is now four lanes. The extra two were built in Japan, towed to Auckland and attached to the sides of the existing bridge. No new pilings needed. Clever, what?

No.: is the written or printed symbol for NUMBER. # will not be understood.

no tipping: You will often see signs that say 'no tipping' in the countryside. These do not enjoin you from presenting honoraria to wandering sheep but rather FORBID the DUMPING of garbage at that point. No tipping signs are not seen in places of business because as a general rule Kiwis do not tip (TIP = to insure promptness). A few of the more expensive restaurants, particularly in the Auckland area have adopted this pernicious habit under the influence of overseas visitors, but those of us who live in N.Z. full time would rather *this did not spread!* (see: *tip, false friends*)

Noodlum: the name of A moderately successful RACEHORSE (gallops, not trots) also MULDOON (the Prime Minister) SPELLED BACKWARDS. (see: *Muldoon, Piggy, gallops, trots, Prime Minister, P.M.*)

Normal School: Unlike the U.S. where Normal School is the old name for Teachers' Colleges, in New Zealand it is the name applied to some PRIMARY SCHOOLS. (see: *Teachers College, false friends*)

North Island: New Zealand consists of a large number of islands. The three major ones are (from north to south) the North Island, the South

Island and Stewart Island. The North Island is the second largest in area (44,190 sq. miles), has the biggest population (2,268,393, 1976 census, people, not sheep) and boasts climates ranging from sub-tropical in the far north to temperate (mild) as you go further south. Then there is windy Wellington! (see: *mainland, South Island, Stewart Island, Auckland, South Auckland, Bay of Plenty, East Coast, Taranaki, Hawkes Bay, Wellington*)

northerly: The WARM WIND from the north. Things are topsy-turvy here with the weather getting warmer (sub tropical even; after all New Zealand is 1000 miles from north to south) as you go north and colder as you go south. Consequently, the northerly is warm and the southerly is cold! (see: *southerly, northern exposure, southern exposure, backwards*)

northern exposure: This is the way you want your HOUSE to FACE, toward the NORTH and the sun. Otherwise, it can be a very chilly place indeed. Because the earth just doesn't tilt far enough, the sun never shines from the south, and with central heating a rarity, the direction of the sun is very important in siting your home. (see: *southern exposure, northerly, southerly, central heating, backwards*)

Northland: the northernmost part of the North Island; above Kaipara Harbour and the city of Wellsford. Northland has 107,013 people (1976), 1,982,000 sheep and 991,000 cattle. Sub-tropical climate, heavy Maori population, beautiful country, superb deep sea fishing, but has a relatively high proportion of rural poor. (see: *North Island*)

not really: means **I don't have the faintest idea.** 'Do you know the way to Purakanui?' 'Not really'. In the United States, this would imply that you had some notion of where the place is and, if you had to, might be able to puzzle out how to get there. In New Zealand, it is likely to mean that you have never heard of Purakanui. (see: *false friends*)

not the full quid: A quid is a pound(£), the currency used in New Zealand until 1967. Something less than a full quid would be a few cents short. If something or someone is not the full quid, they are short of some sense. 'Charlie's not the full quid'. NOT TOO BRIGHT, our Charlie. 'That story the mayor told is not the full quid'. He's HOLDING OUT on us. (see: *declimatization, bob, pound, shilling*)

noughts and crosses: TIC-TAC-TOE.

number 8 fencing wire: The traditional 5 wire fence on New Zealand farms is made with this stuff. In consequence it is one of the things that is always available round a farm when you need to build or repair something. It is said that some cockies can put together a landrover, a tractor and half a milk shed with nothing but a roll of number 8. Wire comes in sizes ranging from 1 to approx. 64, with 1 being the thickest. Number 8 is $\frac{5}{32}$ of an inch or about half the diameter of a pencil. (see: *cocky, Heath-Robinson apparatus, Taranaki Gate*)

N.Z.B.C.: N. Zed B.C. or NEW ZEALAND BROADCASTING CORPORATION. The former (and still commonly used) name for the B.C.N.Z. or Broadcasting Corporation of New Zealand. (see: *B.C.N.Z., national programme, concert programme, wireless, zed*)

N.Z.R.: NEW ZEALAND RAILWAYS Department. The government Department that operates the railroads. I recommend a trip the length of the country by train. It is one of the most spectacular and least comfortable (with the exception of the crack trains the Blue Streak and the Silver Star in the North Island) ways to see New Zealand. Something you will be happy you have done, but won't repeat. N.Z.R. is noted for its coffee. Your first and last sip is said to be a memorable experience. This is a government monopoly protected by strictures on road cartage and by subsidies which allow them to undercut coastal shipping. A pity, because the latter should logically be a lot cheaper to operate for cartage purposes. (see: *M.O.W.*)

O

o(h): What you call the number that is 1 less than 1, especially when talking to a telephone operator. ZERO. (see: *telephone dials*)

odd bod: An *extra person* or one who differs from the norm but not in any inappropriate way. 'We've got nine for dinner, where are we going to put the odd bod?' 'Seven people choose the steak, and two odd bods decided to have chicken instead.' (see: *bod*)

odds and sods: ODDS AND ENDS.

(to come) off the turnips: a Southland expression referring to SOMEONE FRESH FROM THE FARM. (see: *Southland*)

offsider: ASSOCIATE. Could be partner, usually subordinate.

oh yeah: Various meanings ranging from 'IS THAT SO' to 'WHO CARES'. (see: *wouldn't have a clue*)

old boy: MALE ALUMNUS of an educational institution, usually a high school. (see: *old boy network*)

old boy network: originally referred to the unofficial line of communication between graduates of the same (exclusive?) high school. The term is somewhat more plebeian now, referring to any unofficial lines of communication between old friends, often bypassing the mechanisms designed to ensure that everyone is treated the same. (see: *old boy*)

old identity: someone who's been around a long time. 'An old Wellington identity'.

oldies: ANYONE OVER 21, when a teenager is talking. People with teenagers often find themselves referring to themselves and their contemporaries as 'oldies'.

ombudsman: New Zealand has an OFFICIAL who is CHARGED WITH evaluating and if necessary, REDRESSING WRONGS done to individuals by central, and now local, government. If you have a beef, you document it and send it to the ombudsman. It's a brave (and foolish) government department that attempts to flout his rulings.

on remand: in gaol or mental hospital, AWAITING TRIAL. (see: *gaol*)

on the game: the game is PROSTITUTION. Criminal jargon.

on the ice: a drink that is on the ice doesn't necessarily, or even probably, have ice in it, but rather it is being refrigerated.

on the never-never: PURCHASING ON TIME PAYMENT. (see: *hire purchase, lay-by*)

on the pig's back: perhaps because pork is New Zealand's most expensive domestic meat, to 'live on the pig's back' is to LIVE very WELL indeed.

*on the piss: 'He's on the piss, in fact he's been on the piss for four hours'. He's DRINKING (usually beer), in fact . . . (see: *piss, beer*)

on the tiles: If you have been OUT PARTYING all night you have been out on the tiles.

on with: 'Sally and Sam are on with each other'. They enjoy the benefits of the marriage bed without benefit of clergy. (see: *have it off, shag, get one away, stuff, root,* (a) *naughty, bit of crumpet*)

(a) oncer: something that is NOT going TO BE REPEATED. 'This offer of a beautiful color TV for only $1000 is a oncer. Take advantage of it now or never'.

O.N.O.: When you see these letters (sometimes printed as ono) at the end of an advertisement, they invite you to make a bid. $500 ono means $500 OR NEAREST OFFER.

Opera House: Most towns of any size have an Opera House. These are used for most kinds of stage performances but almost all have a resident (amateur) opera company which will stage at least one opera each season. (see: *Dress Circle, flicks, Concert Chamber, theatre, Town Hall*)

orange chocolate chip ice cream: Yummy! Orange colored, orange flavored ice-cream with chocolate chips scattered through it. My New Zealand favorite (all right, so it isn't blueberry cheesecake ice cream). New Zealand ice cream is rich (taste, ingredients) and cheap ($).

ordinary ice cream: VANILLA.

Otago: Have you ever wondered where the 49'ers went when they gave up on finding gold in California? A goodly number of them came to the newly discovered goldfields of Otago (a corruption of the Maori name for one small village). Otago exists on two levels. The relatively flat area near the east coast and the mountain and lake country stretching inland and all the way to the west coast. Dunedin (the old Celtic name for Edinburgh) is the major city (metropolitan area population 120,426 in 1976) and the very large Mc and Mac section of its phone book attests to its Scots heritage, as do the proliferation of pipe (bagpipe) bands in the city and other parts of Otago. The lake country centering around Queenstown is, to my mind, some of N.Z.'s most striking and beautiful country. Otago has (1976 census) 188,903 people, 8,042,000 sheep and 411,000 cattle. (see: *South Island*)

outdoor basketball: the old name for netball. (see: *netball*)

oven tray: COOKIE SHEET. That flat piece of metal on which one bakes cookies. (see: *biscuit, cookie*)

overdraft: The amount by which you have overdrawn your bank account. NEGATIVE $.

overseas funds: Anyone else's currency. New Zealand $ (in denominations larger than $5) are worth very little overseas; as N.Z. does not allow their reimportation. This means that if a company or individual wants to purchase anything from overseas they must obtain some HARD CURRENCY acceptable in the country of origin. Government controls on the availability of such funds are very strict and get stricter as N.Z.'s tendency to import more than it exports (in dollar values) grows. So buy

New Zealand beef and lamb when you get home! Not only will you save money and eat well but you'll help us pay for such luxuries from the U.S. as Yank tanks. (see: *Yank tanks, primary products*)

overstayers: You could be eligible for this obnoxious appellation, although it usually gets hung on Pacific Islanders who have come to work in N.Z. An overstayer is someone who has not left the country when his visa expires. New Zealand's economy, while not buoyant by world standards (see: *terms of trade*) is very good when compared with many of her Pacific neighbors. As a result their citizens would prefer to be in N.Z. where there is work, or welfare payments, instead of at home where both are in very short supply. The Immigration Department has gotten some indignant headlines by raiding houses before dawn to catch these unfortunates. However, as N.Z.'s own unemployment rate worsens, public sympathy for overstayers wanes.

own-your-own: CONDOMINIUM.

owsidgawn: HOW IS IT GOING? a friendly greeting/inquiry. (see: *eryaguan, gidday*)

P

pack a sad: to GET ostentatiously DEPRESSED. (see: *do a Hollywood*)

paddocks: ALL FIELDS, not just those in which horses are kept. (see: *manure*)

pakeha: WHITE MAN in Maori. Weird word because Maori means man. My own guess is that it means 'the ghost that walks'. After a New Zealand winter, Europeans are pale! It is coming to mean native born WHITE New Zealander or KIWI (see: *Kiwi*) in the same way a Sabra is a native born Israeli.

Pa = house)
keha = flea) House flea?

panel beaters: In New Zealand, a young man not born to the farm can ensure his financial and social success by entering one of two equally honorable and lucrative professions. The first is medicine (entered through Medical School) and the second is AUTOMOBILE BODY SHOP work (entered through a 4-7.5 year apprenticeship). On the whole, I recommend the latter, as the responsibilities are slightly lighter and the pay (after apprenticeship) slightly better if you own your own business. (see: *M.B., Ch.B.*)

park: The place where one parks a car is called a park (I'm looking for a park) and there are National parks, but city and country parks are not called parks. (see: *reserve, domain, car park*)

Parliament: The legislative branch of government in N.Z. It consists of 29 representatives of the South Island, a proportional number of North Island seats (North Island population) ÷ (South Island population) plus four Maori seats (North, South, East and West and always Labour Party) making a grand total of 92 M.P.'s. There is only one house (unicameral legislature as in some U.S. states) and no constitution. Theoretically then there is no legal constraint on Parliament preventing it from passing any laws it wishes no matter how liberal or repressive. Somehow this dire possibility never comes to pass. Parliament has three parties in it (1978) one of which (Social Credit) has only one representative. If you listen to Parliament on the radio it quickly becomes obvious that party discipline is much stronger than in the U.S. Congress. This means that the Bills of the majority party pass (always) the Bills of the minority party don't pass (never) and private members' Bills pass (.0001% of the time, i.e. once in living memory). So where are the decisions made? (see: *caucus, National Party, Prime Minister, boys on the hill, shadow cabinet ministers, M.P., Social Credit Party*)

passbook: Your passbook is your BANKBOOK recording your savings account transactions.

Patricia Bartlett: Should anyone who knows England well read this, I'll say that she is New Zealand's Mary Whitehouse. For North Americans, she is rather harder to explain for, while there are many local equivalents, I don't know of any national ones. Patricia Bartlett is the founder of 'The Society for the Promotion of Community Standards' — a group who appear to feel that their extremely high personal morality and wisdom enable them to read all new books, view all new movies and decide which of these are safe for the perusal of us weaker types. Pat Bartlett herself is a poised, witty lady who holds her own well when debating with some of New Zealand's more acerbic figures before largely unsympathetic University audiences. My admiration for the lady does not extend to her cause. New Zealand does have an official film censor (who, in my opinion, rather overdoes it) and a censorship board for books. This latter board, while repugnant in principle, is somewhat less bluenosed in practice. (see: *flicks, X rated*)

pav or **pavlova:** In the 1920's Anna Pavlova came to New Zealand for the first time and floated across the stage into the Kiwi's heart. As a result (so legend has it) THE NATIONAL DESSERT, a feather light concoction made of egg white, sugar and love was named after her. The best of these to my mind, have a marshmallow texture inside and a very light crust outside. If you aren't lucky enough to have some proud Kiwi housewife to invite you in for a bit of the homemade, then I would recommend a commercially made pavlova made by *Cowells*. (These are available in Wellington and Dunedin). By the way, should you visit Australia, you may hear a totally unfounded rumor that this delicious confection is really a native born Australian. While a totally objective culinary historian might feel that there is as much truth in this claim as there is in the New Zealand one, like any other resident of New Zealand, I can assure you that this is pure balderdash and that the pavlova was conceived and rose in Godzone. (see: *Aussie, Godzone*)

pavement: The SIDEWALK is called the pavement. A paved road is called a sealed road. 'Seal begins' and 'seal ends' are common signs, indicating that you are about to run out of or into metal. (see: *seal, metal*)

P.A.Y.E.: PAY AS YOU EARN. That portion of your income tax skimmed off your salary before it ever reaches you. (see: *Inland revenue*)

pea, pie and pud (rhymes with mud): A full meal, a MEAT PIE with a side order of PEAS and MASHED POTATOES. (see: *dressed pies, meat pie, pud*)

Pebbles: With a capital letter, this is one of the brand names for what are known as M&M's in North America. (see: *Smarties*)

peckish: 'Around six o'clock I get peckish, no matter how much I've eaten during the day'. HUNGRY.

Peerless Sheep Nuts: This sign on the side of the road is advertising neither 'mountain oysters' nor the instant answer to virility problems—it is merely one more brand of animal feed. (see: *Feed Moose, mountain oyster*)

penalty kick: awarded by the referee to the side that wasn't caught doing something against the rules in a rugby game. (3 points). (see: *football or footie*)

penny: A penny is not a cent. Penny is a term that refers to the old £ (pounds), s (shillings), d (pence), system that New Zealand used to use. A penny is a large copper coin (about the size of a current 50¢ piece). It is still in use in some lodging houses and motorcamps where they have coin meters on the cooking and/or water heating gas. In these cases, the proprietor will undoubtedly sell you some. A cent, on the other hand is one hundredth of a dollar and the smallest New Zealand coin in both size and value. (see: *decimalization, pound, quid, bob, shilling, sixpence, motorcamp, false friends*)

period: of TIME or menstruation. This is not a form of punctuation. (see: *full stop, false friends*)

perks: PERQUISITES. Those extra advantages that accompany most jobs such as the ability of department store employees to purchase from their own store at a discount, or a salesman's expense account. I know these are innocuous ones, but I don't want to queer anyone's pitch.

petrol: Petrol is GASOLINE, it comes in Super (96 octane), and Regular (86 octane). Almost any passenger vehicle you might operate will use super only. Petrol is sold by liters. Prices are set by government regulation on data submitted by the petrol companies. Consequently, every petrol station, irrespective of brand, or degree of service (service is usually very good) will sell at exactly the same price. The current (Jan. 1980) prices are: Super: 43¢ a liter, or $1.63 per U.S. gallon; Regular: 41.5¢ a liter, or $1.57 per U.S. gallon. If you hear someone talking about gallons or miles per gallon, he is not talking about the U.S. gallon, but rather the Imperial gallon which is $\sim \frac{1}{5}$ larger, (see: *gallon, litre*)

phone box: PHONE BOOTH.

physician: a medical practitioner specializing in the practice of internal medicine. It does not refer to any other kind of medical man. (see: *false friends*)

piddle around or **puddle about:** fiddle around or POTTER ABOUT. (see: *fart arsing around, muck around*)

pie-cart: a house trailer fixed up as a TRAVELING KITCHEN dispensing meat pies (and often fish and chips, dim sims and anything else that can be fried) through a hatch running the entire length of one side. My favorite pie-cart is in Dunedin. It is called the 'Cafe de Curb'. (see: *meat pie, fish and chips, dim sims*)

pig island: wild pigs abound in the wilder places of both the North and

South Islands. It is speculated that they are descendents of swine released by Captain Cook on his voyages of discovery. Despite this illustrious ancestry, neither island seems to wish to claim the name. Just as the residents of both islands wish (for very good reasons) their island to be called the mainland, they are more than willing to pass the pig island name on to the rival land mass. (see: *mainland, North Island, South Island*)

Piggy: The current (1979) PRIME MINISTER'S NICKNAME acquired while the Minister of Finance (in charge of income taxes among other things) in a previous government. He now holds both posts, Prime Minister and Minister of Finance. Mr Robert Muldoon is, and was, an exponent of fiscal restraint. The nickname was presumably imposed by those who felt so restrained. An astute politician, he has decided 'if you can't lick 'em, join 'em' and when approached by a toy manufactuer who wished to put out a line of 'Piggy Banks' which are hollow busts of the Prime Minister, he agreed. The busts are a good likeness, including his famous dimple. One (presumable) deviation from representational art is the coin slot in the head of each bank. Previous recent Prime Ministers also have their nicknames e.g. Big Norm for Norman Kirk (recently deceased), Gentleman Jack (Jack Marshall) and Kiwi Keith for Keith Holyoake (now the Governor-General). (see: *Muldoon, P.M., Prime Minister, Minister of Finance, Noodlum, Governor General*)

pike out: Usually to quit drinking beer before your friends are willing to admit they have reached their capacity. It can refer to PUTATIVE PREMATURE CESSATION of other ACTIVITIES (see: *piker, beer*)

pikelets: A small pancake (like a silver dollar pancake) usually served cold, topped with butter, jam or whipped cream to accompany morning or afternoon tea. The English call these griddle scones or scotch pancakes. (see: *tea, scone*)

piker: Someone who gives up when you aren't ready to. 'Sam's a piker, he piked out when it actually came to stealing the Bobby's hat and I had to do it all by myself. Send bail money'. (see: *pike out, Bobby*)

pilchers: BABIES PLASTIC PANTS (see: *dummy, mac*)

pillowslip: PILLOWCASE.

pinny: What you wear to keep your clothes clean while cooking or washing up, a pinafore or APRON.

*piss: Usually BEER, always booze. (see: *on the piss, beer, pissed, plonk*)

*piss in: SUCCEED. Sam will piss in on that exam (job, race, etc.) (see: *piss in the hand, in the hand*)

*piss in the hand: EASY, usually applied to exams. (see: *piss in, in the hand*)

*piss off: (A) An instruction given to someone whose presence you no longer desire

(B) to MAKE ANGRY.

*pissed, pissed as a newt: DRUNK, bombed, stinko etc. A Friday and Saturday night enterprise on the part of a segment of the community. This is the only country I've ever been to where beer is delivered in tank trucks (like gas trucks) that hold 3024 gallons. They just pump the beer into great vats under each hotel. The Kiwi and the Aussie have a great

77

capacity for beer. The first American Airlines plane into this area ran out of beer within its first hour of flight. This word is not to be confused with pissed off, which means the same as it does in the States (U.S.): angry. (see: *skinful, half cut, piss, brassed off, beer, hotel*)

playcentre: A private co-operative KINDERGARTEN subsidised by Government but administered and taught by parents. Some of these parents receive special training to be paid 'playcentre supervisors'. Children usually attend 2-3 half days per week. (see: *kindy*)

playing gooseberry: being the third that makes a crowd.

plonk — booze: FIREWATER, piss. Usually, however, refers to the national beverage, beer. (see: *beer, piss, pissed*)

Plunket Society: Formed in 1907 under the leadership of Dr Truby King to cut New Zealand's then abnormally high infant mortality rate, this is one of a number of quasi governmental (finance) volunteer agencies that provide many of New Zealand's social services. Plunket provides pre-natal classes in most centers, and has a building/clinic staffed by specially trained 'Plunket Nurses' in most centers. The nurse will visit the new Mum and baby once a week for the first three post-natal months. During the next three months Mum is expected to bring baby into the 'Plunket Rooms' once a week and after that, one visit a month suffices to keep track of baby's height, weight and general health. One tourist note, the cleanest and most convenient ladies toilets in most towns are located in the Plunket Rooms. (see: *Acclimatization Society*)

pluty: 'a very pluty neighborhood'. A very ritzy neighbourhood, or a very WEALTHY one. It is a contraction of plutocratic.

P.M.: It can mean afternoon, but it's more likely to mean PRIME MINISTER. (see: *Prime Minister, Muldoon, Boys on the Hill, M.P., Piggy*)

pohutukawa: (see:) NEW ZEALAND CHRISTMAS TREE. A weather predictor, like the woodchuck, Maori legend has it that if the red blossoms appear early (e.g. November) a long hot summer is in store. (see: *seasons*)

pointsman: Traffic COP DIRECTING TRAFFIC. He points — you go. The Road Code provides for special signals to tell him which way you would like to go. You may or may not get your wish. (see: *M.O.T.*)

pom — pommie: A ruddy (BLOODY? op.cit.) ENGLISHMAN. Many of the Kiwis you will meet are really pommies in disguise. Since my ear isn't fine-tuned enough to distinguish the accents, I must discriminate on the volume of beer they drink (less than the native born). Another distinctive trait is calling England 'home' whether they have been in New Zealand 20 minutes or 20 years. They can't understand why Kiwi's don't do the same, and Kiwis can't understand why they should. Note, however, that the ambition of almost every young Kiwi (see: *Kiwi*) is to visit England.

poncey: behaviour resembling that expected of a male homosexual. (see: *homosexuality, pouf*)

pong: to exude odiferous particles. After a day on the tennis courts or in the glasshouse, I pong. Smell isn't strong enough, STINK comes closer! (see: *glasshouse*)

pontoon: If someone invites you to play a game of pontoon don't look at him blankly or get out your diving gear. He is suggesting a game of

BLACKJACK, or 21. Check local rules before commencing play (e.g. 5 cards under pays ? Is the 10 the equivalent of a face card for passing the deal, etc.)

poozling: Going through abandoned houses scheduled for demolition and removing the (usually antique) fittings that strike your fancy. Until recently this was a socially acceptable practice (although not strictly legal), however, as demolition contractors catch on to the value of these fittings legal and moral pressure is exerted to discourage the practice. SCAVENGING.

pop in: (A) 'I'm going to pop in on Sam'. I'm going to STOP BY and see Sam. (B) 'Pop this in the pot'. PUT this IN the pot. (see: *pop out, pop over, pop on*)

pop on: 'I'm going to pop the kettle on (the stove)'. I'm going to PUT the kettle ON. (see: *pop in, pop out, pop over*)

pop out: 'I'm going to pop out to the dairy'. I'm GOING OUT to the dairy'. (see: *pop in, pop on, pop over, dairy*)

pop over — pop around: 'Pop over some time.' COME VISIT some time. 'Pop around to Uncle Joe's and see how he is.' GO OVER to Uncle Joe's and . . .

(to) post: A method of raising and lowering oneself in rhythm with the gait of the horse you are riding so as to ensure a smooth forward progression. The preceding is true but totally irrelevant. In New Zealand to post is to MAIL, the post is the mail, and the postie is the mailman. (see: *postie, Post Office, call, G.P.O.*)

Post Office: The POST OFFICE is just what it says, but it is also the TELEPHONE COMPANY, the TELEGRAPH COMPANY, a BANK, the place that issues T.V. LICENSES, acts as a LOTTERY AGENT and organizer, does automobile registration, etc., etc. Probably the agency of the government that has the most frequent contact with the populace. In general it is efficient and popular. How's that for a government agency? (see: *television licence, Bonus Bonds, tolls, Prospector's Right*)

postie: That man, or more likely woman in the grey shorts or slacks riding her bicycle (in flat towns like Palmerston North or Christchurch) or striding up and down hills (Wellington, Dunedin, etc.) with mailbag slung over shoulder. For the men, at least, a jersey (which see) is added to the costume. In case my description hasn't rung any bells, it's your friendly neighborhood MAILPERSON. (see: *post, post office, G.P.O.*)

pottle: The South Island term for a SMALL CONTAINER. Originally applied to the little wooden boxes in which berry fruit was sold, it then transferred to the plastic boxes which replaced them. A further extension of the term applied it to small plastic containers of yoghurt and sour cream. (see: *punnet, chip*)

potty: The MINIATURE TOILET upon which very young children are first encouraged to wee and pooh. (see: *wees and poohs, Potty Party*)

Potty Party: One of a large number of small political parties that spring up at election time and then disappear forever, or for at least three years. Others are The Imperial British Conservative Party (see: (the) *Wizard of Christchurch*), The Garden Party and the (see:) *Fred Dagg* Party. They do liven up an election. (see: *potty, National Party, Labour Party, Values Party, Social Credit Party*)

pouf or **poufter:** (A) QUEER. As in homosexual, this meaning probably comes from a female hair fashion, popular in England in the 1700's. (see: *poncy, homosexuality*)

    (B) pouf can also refer to an OTTOMAN on which you rest your feet. This may derive from that same hair fashion since it involved building up the hair on top of the head into a thick mattress. (see: *humpty, scats*)

pound: (A) 453 grams. The unit of measure that you and I, and most Kiwis are used to. However in 1976 N.Z. got completely metricated and we've all been confused since. (see: *metrication*)

    (B) Before 1967 N.Z.'s monetary unit (equivalent to $2 NZ). In 1967 N.Z. got decimalized. This confusion is slowly clearing up as the younger generation grows. (see: *decimalization, not the full quid, shilling, bob, as silly as a two-bob watch, false friends*)

pozzie: A location in space or a POSITION. 'I've got a good pozzie for the races — you can see everything.'

P.P.T.A.: Not a strange version of the P.T.A. but the rather militant SECONDARY SCHOOL TEACHERS' UNION, the Post Primary Teachers Association (see: *college*)

pram: A BABY BUGGY. A shortened version on perambulator. You will see a series of hooks attached to the front of city buses. These hooks are there so that you can hang your pram on the outside of the bus before getting in with babe in arms. Provides more room all round. (see: *sulky, pushchair*)

prang: That's what you had better not do to the boss' car when you borrow it. BANG UP, DENT or otherwise reduce from pristine glory to mundane mediocrity. Usually used in reference to automobiles.

prawn: An expression largely confined to Southland. It implies a certain deficiency in cognitive skills in the individual so described. DUMMY. (see: *Southland*)

prefect: SCHOOL MONITOR. (see: *head prefect*)

primary products: New Zealand's economic lifeline. Primary products are the animal, horticultural and grain PRODUCE of New Zealand farms. Two-thirds or more of the overseas funds earned by N.Z. come from the export of this produce. This is extremely important in a modern country that provides less than 1% of its own oil needs etc. etc. (see: *overseas funds, sheep, terms of trade, freezing workers, wharfies*)

primary school: ELEMENTARY SCHOOL (see: *school*)

Prime Minister: The POLITICAL but not the titular HEAD of the N.Z. GOVERNMENT. This position is held by the elected (by his colleagues) leader of the majority party in Parliament. He is also the representative of an electoral district. A strong Prime Minister can pretty well get whatever legislation he likes passed. The present (1979) Prime Minister represents an electoral district near Auckland called Tamaki. He is a strong P.M.! (see: *P.M., Muldoon, Piggy, boys on the hill, Parliament, caucus*)

private hotel: (see: *hotel*)

privates: (A) The lowest rankers in the army.

(B) That portion of your anatomy whose public exposure could lead to public censure. (see: *short and curlies, minge, crutch-crutching, false friends*)

Privy Council: The Supreme Court in New Zealand isn't supreme and the highest N.Z. court, the Appeals Court, isn't supreme either. Cases can be appealed once more to the Crown or more specifically to the Judicial Committee of the Monarch's Privy Council in London. Like the U.S. Supreme Court the Privy Council reserves the right to select which of the cases appealed to it will actually be heard. The Judicial Committee of the Privy Council is made up of 'eminent Judges of Commonwealth countries'. The apron strings aren't all that slack as yet! (see: (the) *Queen, Supreme Court*)

problems: There is a tendency to take professional criticism very personally in New Zealand. One American friend was hired as a consultant to a government department and sent around the country to see what she could do to help the various branches of this department. When talking to the people in each new branch she initially would say, 'What kind of problems are you having with . . .?' This produced an immediate clam up. After much frustration, she hit upon this formula, 'What particular challenges are you facing here?' This immediately elicited the list of problems that she was after.

procession: A procession is a PARADE. Every town in New Zealand finds an excuse for at least one of these each year, complete with floats, queens, brass bands, bagpipe bands, etc. etc. The term applies to other kinds of parades, for instance, students and staff marching to the graduation ceremony form a procession. (see: *capping*)

Professor: In an American University everyone is a Professor. So much so that Dr. is the title of choice. In N.Z. things are very different. Until very recently one wasn't a professor, one was 'the Professor of . . .', in other words the DEPARTMENT HEAD. In these prosperous days a university department may boast two or even three 'Chairs' (one for each Professor) while the lower ranks are Associate Professors-Readers, Senior Lecturers, Lecturers, and Junior Lecturers. Consequently low ranked American academics who reply to the inevitable status question that they are Assistant Professors find themselves receiving unwonted deference. (see: *Chair, Reader, Associate Professor, Lecturer, false friends*)

programme: PROGRAM. (see: *gaol, nett, Words*)

Proms: This has nothing to do with the senior prom. They are instead a series of CONCERTS given annually throughout the country by the New Zealand (Broadcasting Corporation) National (Symphony) Orchestra. (see: *BCNZ, ball, false friends*)

property: A property is usually a BUILDING, and its surrounding ground. It may be a residence or a commercial building. 'That's a nice property you have there.' 'That's a nice house (building etc.) you have there.' This usage survives in the U.S. in 'Get off my property'. (see: *section*)

Prospectors Right: Purchased for $2 from the Post Office or the Department of Mines this entitles you to:

(a) 'Enter on unoccupied Crown (i.e. government owned) land and prospect and conduct tests for any mineral'

(c) 'Keep . . . samples . . . of any mineral found . . .' This is what entitles you to go gold panning in central Otago. Tremendously exciting when you see your first flashes of 'colour'. (see: *Otago*)

P.S.A.: The PUBLIC SERVICE ASSOCIATION is the UNION OF GOVERNMENT EMPLOYEES (68,000 members). Not given to taking (see:) industrial action, it nevertheless is one of the most successful unions in the country when it comes to negotiating pay rises to keep pace with inflation. This success may be partially attributed to the fact that governments don't spend their own money. (see: *F.O.L., industrial action, industrial unrest*)

pseuds: As in people who taste the label, and not the wine.

pubbing: My unmarried North Island friends tell me this is the latest term for USING your local watering hole AS a SINGLES BAR. (see: *hotel*)

public bar: No chairs, no women (ladies?), no carpet, scattered high tables, dart board, oceans of beer. This NO FRILLS BAR is found in licensed hotels along with the more luxurious lounge bar. However, 'times they are a changing' and even the most traditional of public bars now has scattered a few high stools around and reluctantly admits those few women who venture in. (see: *hotel, lounge bar, licensed hotel, booze barn, six o'clock swill, tavern, beer*)

public holidays: New Zealand is not deficient in these, and shops observe them religiously. The approximate dates of the major ones are indicated below, however, for some of these (non religious holidays), if they fall on a weekend or midweek they may be moved to the nearest Monday or Friday to provide a long weekend.

NATIONAL HOLIDAYS

January 1 & 2	— New Years
February 6	— Waitangi (N.Z.) day
Easter time	— Good Friday
	— Easter Monday
April 25	— ANZAC day
1st Mon. in June	— Queen's Birthday
December 25	— Christmas Day
December 26	— Boxing Day

Provincial Holidays (celebrated on the nearest Monday)

Wellington	— January 22
Auckland	— January 29
Northland	— January 29
Nelson	— February 1
Taranaki	— May 31
Otago/Southland	— March 23
Hawkes Bay	— A & P Show Day
Marlborough	— November 1
Canterbury	— December 16
Westland	— December 1

(see: *Waitangi day, ANZAC day, Queen's Birthday, Boxing Day*)

pud or **pudding:** That sweet taste at the end of the meal, whether or not it is a pudding. In fact, DESSERT is most likely to be fruit salad (with or without ice cream). (see: *pav*)

puffed: Tired, BEAT, worn out. 'After running up those twelve flights of stairs I'm puffed.' Descriptive isn't it?

puha: A native (Maori) SPINACH. Very tasty with a white sauce.

*puke: REGURGITATE. (see: *Technicolor yawn, spew*)

punched out: BEATEN UP. (see: *punch-up*)

punch-up: A bout of fisticuffs not bounded by Marquis of Queensberry rules, and often occurring on the eve of the Sabbath in the confines of a place in which spirituous liquors are purveyed. FIGHT. (see: *punched out, get your face smacked in, hotel*)

puncture: FLAT tire.

punnet: The North Island term for a SMALL BOX OF BERRIES, e.g. strawberries. (see: *pottle, chip*)

punter: GAMBLER, usually on the horses. (see: *punting, trots, gallops, T.A.B., false friends*)

punting: Not ordinarily poling a boat or kicking a football but rather PLACING A BET. (see: *trots, gallops, punter, T.A.B., false friends*)

pushbike: The kind of bike that you push along by pressing (alternately) upon the pedals. A BICYCLE. A bike is something else again. (see: *bike, motorbike*)

pushchair: A much more logical name for a baby's STROLLER. (see: *pram, sulky*)

pussy: Has no salacious connotations! A pussy is a cat, in fact this is the exact equivalent of KITTY. When calling his cat at night instead of calling 'kitty-kitty-kitty' a Kiwi calls 'puss-puss-puss' or 'pussy-woosy-woosy', if you are like one of my wives who shall (otherwise) remain nameless. (see: *cat*)

put the hard word on: To INSIST that a difficult DECISION be MADE. Usually used in the context of pressuring someone to grant sexual favors or, 'put their money where their mouth is' in the case of a business deal or an offer of marriage. (see: *on with*)

put the wind up: Much as it sounds that way, this is not a euphemism for eructation. (see: *break wind*) 'The Inland Revenue really put the wind up Sam when they demanded copies of all his receipts for last year.' The Internal Revenue really FRIGHTENED Sam when... (see: *Inland Revenue*)

pyjamas: PAJAMAS. (see: *Words*)

Q

(the) quack: That practitioner of the medical arts to whom you take your ills. DOCTOR. (see: *M.B., Ch.B.*)

quarter white: Southland term for HALF a 700 gramme LOAF of bread. I know it doesn't make any sense! (see: *bread, Southland*)

(the) Queen: That is, the Queen of New Zealand, who just happens to be the same grand lady who is the Queen of England, Ireland, Wales, Canada, Australia, etc. She gets out here once every five years or so and walks around so she can be looked at. During her absences from New Zealand (i.e. most of the time) she is directly represented by a surrogate called the Governor-General. (see: *Governor-General*)

Every Christmas she broadcasts her message to the Commonwealth which is seen by most people. It invariably starts, 'My husband and I . . .' This stock phrase has become a standing (largely affectionate) joke that is revived every year.

Queen's Birthday: Is celebrated as a PUBLIC HOLIDAY on the 1st MONDAY IN JUNE. The present Queen was born April 21, 1926, Victoria was born May 24, 1819. So whose birthday is it?

Elizabeth II	April 21, 1926
George IV	December 14, 1895
Edward VIII	June 24, 1894
George V	June 3, 1865
Edward VII	November 9, 1841
Victoria	May 24, 1819
William IV	August 21, 1765
George IV	August 12, 1762
George III	June 4, 1738

So it appears that if you are celebrating the 'Queen's Birthday' you are really celebrating either the birthday of George V, a king the world has some reason to respect, or George III, whose reputation rather suffers from history, particularly in the U.S.

In any case a long weekend at the beginning of June makes a nice break in the year and that is probably why the celebration hasn't followed the sovereign's actual birthday. I must admit some personal disappointment at this information as, knowing it wasn't Queen Elizabeth's own birthday, I'd always assumed it was *The Queen* (Victoria) whose birthday we were celebrating. (see: *public holidays*)

quenchers: I'm not sure what is that they are supposed to quench but this is the South Island equivalent of the North Island's (see:) *ice blocks* or the American ICE CUBES.

quid: N.Z.'s pre-1967 unit of currency $2.00 NZ. (see: *POUND, decimalization, not the full quid, shilling, bob*)

quite: (A) If you read a letter of recommendation which said: 'He is really a quite brilliant man,' you are likely to think that the individual in question has one or two grey cells to rub together.

A Kiwi on the other hand, would read that statement as 'He is of mediocre intellect.' When used to modify something good, quite means NOT VERY. When used to modify something discreditable, it does mean very. 'Sam is quite a bad sort.' Sam is a very bad man. This is then a subtle and very dangerous false friend, particularly when someone's future rides on your word. (see: *false friends*)

(B) It is also used as an affirmation of someone else's statement. 'Bazzer's a good man.' 'Quite.' (see: *'story*)

R

Randy: I have sad news for those of you with this fine old American name. If you are Randy Murgatroyd Smith and you have always gone by Randy M. Smith the time has come to give Murgatroyd an airing (or at least Randolph). It's no worse to be called Randy in N.Z. than it would be to be called HORNY in the U.S. Kiwis find this overwhelmingly funny, but you won't. Before ignoring this advice (after all you never could stand Murgatroyd or Randolph) imagine how your kid sister would react to a young man who approached her with this line, 'Hello, I'm Horny, what's your name?'

range: If you were home on the range in N.Z. you might find it a trifle warm, as the range is the KITCHEN STOVE. (see: *false friends*)

rapt — wrapped: Teenage slang for being ENRAPTURED, that is, in love with someone.

rat bag: To call someone a rat bag is to imply that they have done something of which you disapprove. A MILD REBUKE.

rate of knots: To move at the rate of knots is to move with GREAT SPEED. The phrase can be used to refer to activities other than locomotion. For instance, 'Felicity is getting through that box of chocolate at the rate of knots'.

rattle your dags: HURRY ALONG there. (see: *dag*)

Reader: Literacy is assumed, but not required for this position, an academic rank corresponding with a U.S. PROFESSOR (who is not a department head). Another misleading N.Z. name for the same rank is Associate Professor. For those familiar with the English academic system a Reader in N.Z. is not the same as a Reader in England; as it is a teaching position in N.Z. rather than a research title as in England. (see: *Associate Professor, Lecturer, Professor, Chair, false friends*)

Reentry Permit: If you become a resident of New Zealand, but not a citizen, then go to the Department of Labour and Immigration before going overseas on a trip and get one of these. Otherwise the Immigration folks here can be just as bloody minded as their U.S. counterparts and that is very bloody minded indeed. (see: *bloody minded, bloody*)

relief teacher: SUBSTITUTE TEACHER.

reserve: A reserve is a PARK, usually one located in a town or city. (see: *domain, park, city*)

retaining wall: A retaining wall (hopefully) restrains the dirt behind it. This tends to keep that same dirt from coming down and filling your yard and your home, or the public street.

right: Used as an adjective, this adds EMPHASIS WITHOUT MEANING, somewhat like as real is used in the United States. 'Sam is a right twit.' Sam is a real idiot.

right oh or **rightey oh:** OKAY. (see: *jolly dee*)

ring: TELEPHONE or call. (see: *call*)

rissole: It looks like a hamburger, its taste is indescribable but it ain't good.

rock melon: No one will recognize the word CANTALOUPE, but that's what it is.

Roman fingers: High school slang for the digits of a boy who, when juxtaposed to a member of the opposite sex, can't keep his hands to himself.

Upon reading the preceding, a lady friend said that it's really the W.H.B. or 'Wandering Hands Brigade'.

root: (A) Root most often means COPULATE. Therefore Kiwis find an American who says 'I live on route 69' absolutely sidesplitting. (see: *Randy, have it off, have it away, shag, stuff, on with, (a) naughty, bit of crumpet, false friends*)

(B) The underpinnings of a plant.

rough enough: Means CLOSE ENOUGH as in a 'rough enough estimate'.

(a) round: Is a ROUND OF DRINKS, or the purchase by you of one drink for every member of your party. Since it is very impolite to drink other people's booze without shouting your own round it is a good move to buy the first or second round. This enables you to depart gracefully should you find yourself flagging, or wish to depart for some other reason. (see: *shout*)

round the bend — round the twist: This is the corner one is assumed to have turned when your behavior becomes so aberrant that the little men in the white coats are called. INSANE.

R.S.A.: RETURNED SERVICEMEN'S ASSOCIATION. N.Z.'s equivalent of the American Legion.

RSJ: Rolled Steel Joist. The N.Z. name for an I BEAM like those that form the skeletons of skyscrapers.

rubber: Not what you wear on your feet (those are galoshes), not what you wear elsewhere (see: *french letter*), but the bit of gum arabic that you use to remove your pencilled errors. An ERASER.

rubbish: Substitute this word wherever you would normally use the words GARBAGE or TRASH. Hence a garbage can or trash can becomes a rubbish tin. A garbage dump becomes a rubbish tip, etc. (see: *tin* and *tip*)

ruddy: If you are too refined (or inhibited) to say (see:) *BLOODY*, which rates two asterisks, you can swear mildly by saying ruddy. Euphemisms for swear words themselves become guilty by association.

rugby or rugger: N.Z. football, 15 men to a side, 40 min. half, 5 min. half time, spiked boots but no protective clothing. (see: *football, All Blacks, sprigs, hooker*)

run holder: Does this conjure up images of someone successfully re-straining a case of Montezuma's revenge?

A run holder is the LEASE HOLDER on a cattle or sheep station when the government actually owns the land. (see: *high country station, station, sheep station, muster, cocky*)

S

Saaday: The day after Friday. (see: *gidday*)

salesclerk: SALESMAN or SALESGIRL. (see: *clerk, Are you being served?*)

(The) Sallies: Saturday night concerts in the Town square (you can't fault their enthusiasm), good works galore, involved in nearly every worthwhile project designed to help individuals in need in New Zealand. Tamborines, comic opera uniforms and all, the SALVATION ARMY is much more a part of the daily fabric of life in New Zealand than it is in the U.S. They also run a couple of surprisingly good (non-alcoholic) hotels called the People's Palaces. These are clean, cheap, the food is good and they are conveniently located in Auckland and Wellington. Recommended for the budget traveler.

salt and pepper shakers: Another instance where the painstakingly acquired knowledge of a lifetime will totally mislead you. The shaker with one hole (or very few holes) in the top is the salt; the shaker with multiple small holes in the top is the pepper. (see: *backwards*)

sand hill: Those heaps of sand on the beach. A SAND DUNE.

sandfly: The scourge of New Zealand as far as tourists are concerned. Most especially found on the West Coast (of the South Island), these gnat-sized flies swarm like gnats and bite like mosquitoes (the really vicious kind). I recommend the liquid form of an insect repellent called *DIMP*; smear it on all exposed skin surfaces liberally and also put some on reachable surfaces that aren't exposed. Don't let them keep you away from Milford Sound's magnificent scenery, but go prepared! (see: *West Coast*)

sandshoes: TENNIS SHOES (see: *gym boots*)

sandwich: Presumably named after the 4th Earl of Sandwitch famous in other ways. 'For corruption and incapacity, Sandwitch's administration is unique in the history of the British navy.'

James Cook, discoverer of New Zealand, also discovered and named the Sandwich Islands (Hawaiian Islands). Alas, the name didn't stick, but his discovery did. The New Zealand sandwich wouldn't, however, be given houseroom by Dagwood. It consists of what you would consider one slice of bread cut down the middle to make two very thin slices. Between these slices is put one miniscule layer of (usually) a single substance such as a thin slice(s) of tomato or vegemite or marmite. (see: *vegemite, marmite, filled roll, bread rolls, doorstops*)

Saturday paper: In North America the Saturday edition of any daily paper tends to be the thinnest, least imposing and least worthwhile in terms of classified advertisements. In New Zealand, the dailies don't publish on Sunday, so the Saturday paper is the closest equivalent to a North American SUNDAY PAPER and has all the ads and some of the supplements. (see: *backwards, Sunday papers, local rag*)

sausage dog: DACHSHUND. (see: *alsatian*)

saveloy: A banger (SAUSAGE) in disguise, it looks like a fat red hotdog and is an acquired taste. Not recommended. (see: *bangers, alpine sticks*)

savouries: HOT FINGER FOOD that consists of a pastry shell around meat or some other non-sweet, non-dessert food. (see: *savoury pies*)

savoury pies: Hot meat pies, or bacon and egg pies (the latter, apple pie sized, is the most unusual way of serving bacon and eggs). This applies to any kind of non-sweet pie. (see: *meat pies, mince pies, savouries*)

scats: For the North Island this usually refers to thick cushions scattered on the floor to make sitting there comfortable. In the South Island it usually refers to a close relation, the OTTOMAN or footstool. (see: *humpty, pouf*)

school: Is a term that refers to primary and secondary schools only. It does not refer to pre-school education (see: *kindy, playcentre*) or tertiary education (see: *Uni, varsity, Teachers College*)

Primers 1, 2, 3, 4	Ages 5-7
Standards 1, 2, 3, 4	Ages 7-11
Standards 5, 6 or Forms 1, 2	Ages 11-13
Forms 3, 4, 5, 6, 7	Ages 13-18

   (see: *college*)

School Cert: Or School Certificate. Those of you from the Empire State will be familiar with the REGENTS EXAMS. School Certificate exams are national examinations taken at age 15-16 (end of fifth form) by every student. A student elects the subjects in which he wishes to be examined. The passing level is the fiftieth percentile. That means that 50% of the people taking each subject must pass that subject and 50% must fail it. The saving grace is that students take more than one subject (up to six) and can repeat the exam in later years. None the less, to 'have School Cert.' is far from a meaningless statement. You must have been in the top half of examinees in the whole country for your year. As a result no New Zealand high school can be a 'diploma mill'. (see: *U.E., Bursary, school, college, Teachers College*)

school holidays: From MID DECEMBER TO THE END OF JANUARY the kids are on holiday. Consequently most families take their vacation in this period. This means that (unless you are on a package tour) you had better arrange accommodation in advance, even to reserving sites at motor-camps. This of course applies to resort areas; the cities are empty. Also public transportation is heavily booked during this period, so plan early. This also applies to the term breaks in May and August when the kids are let off the hook for 2-3 weeks, depending on their educational level. (see: *January, Christmas, motorcamps*)

school uniform: All secondary school pupils wear uniforms. Independent of climate those in public schools seem to wear (for the boys) grey shorts, grey knee socks and grey V-necked sweaters with green trim around the collar. The girls usually wear the same colors but add a skirt, white blouse and a necktie (there's a role reversal for you). From the fifth form on, things are usually a bit classier, with the older boys in blazers, ties and long pants and the girls in a feminine version of the same.

   I thought this was terrible until hearing a female American Field Scholar (a U.S. high school exchange student) saying that she liked wearing the uniform since it eliminated the clothing competition between girls which she was used to in the U.S. I've been reduced to a position of ambivalence. (see: *school, college*)

scoff: TO EAT RAPIDLY. 'If you keep scoffing down your food like that you'll get an ulcer, or give me one.' (see: *snavel, snarf, false friends*)

scone: An (when hot) utterly delicious BAKING POWDER BISCUIT. Literally melts in your mouth. (see: *biscuit* and *water biscuit*) Occasionally used to refer to one's HEAD as in 'use your scone'.

scratcher or **grunter:** After a long and tiring day when you finally lay your weary bones to rest, you do it on a scratcher. BEDS can of course be used for other activities.

screw: There are good screws and bad screws. Well, a good screw is a large SALARY, and a bad screw is a small one. The word also means what you think it does, so don't use it loosely, but don't assume it refers to sex if you hear it.

script: a PRESCRIPTION. 'Get the doctor to give you a script for some antibiotics'. The script will cost you (50¢ – $1.50) but the drugs themselves are subsidized by the N.Z. government and are usually free.

scrubber: An adolescent GIRL WITH ROUND HEELS; teenage slang. (see: *lusty wench, town bike*)

scrum: An orderly free-for-all in rugby which determines which side gets a ball that is in dispute. (see: *hooker, All Blacks*)

seagulls: (A) Seagulls occupy the social and economic position in New Zealand that pigeons do in North America; although there are usually a few pigeons around trying to make a living off their leavings. It is seagulls that will panhandle you in the park, swarm over the rubbish tip and provide the only reminder of animal life, other than man, downtown. They are, by and large, more aggressive and enterprising beggars than pigeons in that they are most adept at stealing what isn't offered.

(B) a PART TIME or seasonal STEVEDORE on the docks. (see: *wharfie*)

seal: Performing Marineland in Napier. The performing sea leopard is most impressive. Otherwise short for TARSEALED ROAD. (see: *metal, pavement*)

(the) season: The season is for killing. TIME TO SLAUGHTER all of those cattle and sheep that provide steaks and chops for New Zealand and a good chunk of the rest of the world. The season begins October-November, and finishes around June. The further south you go, the later it starts and finishes. Industrial unrest in the freezing works always reaches a peak at the beginning of the season as this is when the freezing workers have the most clout. (see: *freezer, freezing workers, abattoir, works, primary products, terms of trade*)

seasoned topside: BEEF WITH STUFFING (stuffing reminiscent of your last Thanksgiving dinner). (see: *colonial goose, topside*)

seasons: Backwards of course. Summer is December, January and February, one spends Christmas on the beach. Winter is June, July and August, skiing time; March, April and May are Autumn. (Kiwis find the word Fall peculiar in the extreme) and September, October and November are Spring. (see: *Christmas, backwards*)

section: A section is a section of ground or a building LOT. 'You've got a nice section Sam, grow all those shrubs yourself?' (see: *property*)

semi-detached: If you live in a DUPLEX it is 'semi-detached'.

sent down the road: To be relieved of the necessity of returning to your place of employment as a result of involuntary separation from your employer. FIRED.

service: This is provided by bulls for cows and stallions for mares, resulting in calves and foals. Sheep have another word for it. (see: *tupping*)

serviette: What the gentlefolk use at the dinnertable to wipe their mouths after eating. A NAPKIN isn't the same by any other name. (see: *napkin, false friends*)

shadow cabinet ministers: The members of cabinet are those members of the majority party in Parliament, the legislative branch of government, elected by their colleagues, to run the executive branches of government (like making a Senator, Secretary of State).

The PARTY OUT OF POWER also chooses a spokesman for each of these areas. These SPOKESMEN are collectively called the shadow cabinet, just as the spokesmen of the majority party (called Ministers) make up the cabinet. (see: *Parliament, caucus, boys on the hill, Prime Minister, Minister of Finance, National Party, Labour Party*)

shag: (A) to juxtapose a male and female of the human species in such a way that species perpetuation may result if deliberate precautions are not taken. (see: *have it off, get one away, stuff, root, on with, (a) naughty, bit of crumpet*)

(B) 'gidday shag', hi BUDDY (see: *gidday*)

(C) A SEABIRD (cormorant) most subspecies of which have a comical topknot.

shandy: The ladies who don't particularly like alcohol will have a MIXTURE of LEMONADE *(Sprite)* AND BEER when dragged to the hotel. Sounds ghastly, surprisingly doesn't taste half bad. (see: *lemonade, hotel*)

shank's pony: The old grey mare ain't what she used to be (ON FOOT, SHANKS MARE).

sharebroker: The man from Merrill Lynch, Pierce, Fenner and Te Raparaha. Your friendly neighborhood STOCKBROKER.

sharemilker: You own the cattle, I look after them and milk them for a share of the milk or the profit therefrom. A sharemilker is SOMETHING LIKE a TENANT FARMER.

shark and tatties: Another way of saying (see:) *fish and chips* that emphasizes the usual ingredient of the fish segment. Don't turn up your nose; it's good.

she: Replaces IT in all kinds of sentences. 'She's a good old bucket of bolts.' 'She'll be right, mate.' 'She's a cold one today.' (see: *she'll be right*)

she'll be right mate: It has been argued that this is the N.Z. philosophy. In general it suggests 'everything for the best in this best of all possible worlds', and in specific terms it means DON'T WORRY, IT WILL WORK OUT O.K.

sheep: N.Z. has 60,000,000 of these (and 3,000,000 people). The Kiwi economy lives off the sheep's chops, wool, and hides, the rest is window dressing. (Well, there are 12,000,000 cattle). (see: *primary products, overseas funds, terms of trade, freezing works, hogget, two-toothed ewe, a lamb is a sheep before you've carried it very far*)

sheep station: SHEEP FARM (see: *station*)

sheila: A sheila is a FEMALE of the human species. Ah! You've heard that before; but where? Probably from your grandparents or parents since this description was current in North America in the 1920's and 30's. It is everyday speech, neither laudatory or derogatory, like calling a man a bloke.

I have been told by a modern young lady that 'sheila' raises her hackles, 'even if the blokes don't mean to be derogatory'. (see: *bird, bloke, bit of crumpet, bit of fluff*)

shifting: When you transfer your family and worldly goods from one place to another in the U.S. you are MOVING. The same process in New Zealand is called shifting. You might move from one chair to another, but you shift house.

shilling: Occasionally someone will hand you a coin that has shilling written on it, or a friend will ask to borrow a shilling. This used to be 1/20 of a pound in pre-1967 currency; now it is a DIME. (see: *decimalization, pound, quid, bob, sixpence, penny*)

*shit hot: DAMN GOOD.

shoe sizes: I have good news for those of you with big feet! You have smaller feet in New Zealand. In general, New Zealand shoes (made to British lasts) run one size larger than their U.S. counterparts. So if you wear a 13 in the U.S. you wear a 12 in New Zealand. A U.S. 6 is a N.Z. 5, etc.

I have bad news for those of you with big feet! It is damn difficult to get anything but work boots and 1940's brogues in N.Z. size 12's and nearly impossible to find larger sizes.

The ladies may have an additional problem. The British lasts used in New Zealand are designed for feet that are, on average, wider, than the U.S. female foot of equal length. In consequence, the ladies may find themselves faced with a choice of too short, or too wide.

shop: Not usually a workshop but rather a STORE. (see: *shop assistants, sales clerks*)

shop assistant: That's the title of the SALESMAN or SALESLADY who assists you to make your purchases. In many cases, particularly hardware stores, their assistance is real and practical as opposed to merely courteously taking your money. These people are also referred to as sales clerks. (see: *Are you being served?, sales clerk*)

**short and curlies: PUBIC HAIR. I wasn't going to include this one, but when the caption 'The Short and Curly Show' appeared on the marquee of the legitimate theater in Dunedin's octagonal town square, I felt it was truly a term in public usage. This was the name of the annual student capping concert. If it's this public, how can we ignore it? (see: *minge, privates, crutch, capping, capping concert*)

shorts: Bermuda shorts, knee socks, white shirt, jacket and tie are what the well dressed businessman will wear on a summer day. (see: the cover of this book)

shout: A pleasant sound — 'BUY', as in 'I'll shout you a drink' — a most welcome and common phrase in Kiwiland. Shouts are invariably reciprocated and I have been told that shouting a round 'is the best way to get everyone as drunk as possible, as fast as possible'.

It might interest you to know that a 'Yankee shout' means dutch treat.

— Tight anyone? (see: (a) *round*)

shufti: This one came back from North Africa with those New Zealand troops who did make it back. A shufti is a RECONNAISSANCE. 'Let's take a shufti into town and look over that new store.' (see: *dekko*)

side: Remember as a kid choosing up sides for a ball game? Well, this term survives into adulthood in New Zealand where a ball TEAM is more likely to be referred to as the side, than the team. There is a subtle distinction here, in that the All Black team comprises all the players, but the All Black side that played Wales, refers only to those players chosen to play against Wales in that particular match. (see: *All Blacks, test, match, touring*)

sideboards: Them furry things you (men) wore on the side of your face about five years ago. SIDEBURNS are still popular in N.Z.

silly galoot: STUPID IDIOT!

silverbeet: This has nothing to do with what we would normally call beets. It is instead a spinach-like green known in the United States as Swiss chard. (see: *veges, beetroot*)

silverside: A PICKLED (corned?) RUMP ROAST OF BEEF. Yeah, I know, but that's what my butcher said. (see: *topside, seasoned topside, butchery, T-bone*)

singlet: This esoteric garment is an old-fashioned sleeveless UNDERSHIRT. My grandfather used to wear one every day. In N.Z. they come in two major varieties, white and colored (one variety). This is worn under one's shirt for warmth. Without central heating warm clothes to be worn indoors become very important. The second variety of singlet is black. This one is the stereotype farmers' uniform worn without an overshirt while doing any sort of hot work, e.g. shearing, mowing, etc. (see: *Fred Dagg, jersey, spencer, vest*)

sink a few: To CONSUME a number of glasses of BEER. (see: *beer, shout, brew*)

S.I.S.: The Security Intelligence Service, NEW ZEALAND'S C.I.A. Deserved or not, they have the image of ham-fisted clowns in trench coats busy protecting secrets New Zealand hasn't got. The only headline making arrest I can recall was that of a former Permanent Secretary in the Trade and Industry Department who, although no longer working for the Government, was accused of selling trade secrets to the Soviet Union, i.e. he was accused of telling them the lowest price New Zealand would accept for some considerable quantity of meat and wool. Of course, he too, should not have had access to this information but like everywhere else, the old boy network functions very well in New Zealand and it was alleged that the information came to him through that route. He was acquitted. (see: *old boy network*)

sister: This can refer to those of your female relatives with whom you share one or more parents, and it can refer to the black-gowned lady with the white headband who teaches in your local Catholic school; but it is most likely to refer to the (senior) NURSE who binds up your wounds and awakens you at 10.00 p.m. to give you a sleeping pill. (see: *matron*)

six o'clock swill: Prior to 9 October 1967, bars in New Zealand had to close at 6.00 p.m. (now they close at 10.00 p.m., often 12.00 p.m. on weekends and the house bar, for people staying in the hotel, has even more flexible hours). This meant that your average working man had to do his day's drinking between 5 and 6.00 p.m. I've had described to me pubs in which the floor was cement and the front of the bar stainless steel with a bit of a trough at the bottom. After all, if you only have one hour or less to do your day's drinking you don't want to waste time running to the grot. These places were hosed out after six.

As a social necessity then, hotels tended to have public bars for this kind of drinking and ladies and escorts' bars for more civilized tippling. (see: *public bar, lounge bar, hotel, beer, licensed hotel, booze barn, grot*)

sixpence: Is 5¢. This dates back to the days when there were 12 pence to the shilling and 20 shillings to the pound, the New Zealand unit of currency (pre-1967). Came decimalization and shillings were easy to handle since there had been 20 shillings in a pound and a pound was set equal to $2.00 — a shilling naturally became 10¢. However, at 240 pence to the pound no such simple conversion was available for the sixpence. 200 divided by 6 is 33.33 but 200 divided by 5 is 40. So by a process of double-think if all 6d. pieces became 5¢ pieces, all the pieces fall into place. (see: *decimalization, shilling, bob, pound, quid, penny*)

skinful: Of booze. To be DRUNK is to have a skinful. Evocative isn't it? Similarly one can have a skinful of (be fed up with) another person. (see: *pissed, beer, boozer, hotel*)

skip or **mini skip:** A large trash container designed to be lifted and emptied mechanically by a specially equipped truck. Called DUMPSTERS in some parts of the U.S. As a verb, the word means the same as it does in North America. (see: *tip, rubbish, tin, kitchen tidy, false friends*)

skite: (A) BRAG. 'He's always skiting.'

(B) BRAGGART. 'Sam's just a skite. Don't pay any attention to him.'

skungy: 'That's the skungiest looking bloke I ever saw.' That's the most GRUBBY guy I've ever seen.

slack me off — slacked off: ANGER – ANGRY. 'You slack me off the way you go around skiting all the time.' You piss me off the way you go around bragging all the time. 'I've never been so slacked off in my life!' I've never been so angry in my life! (see: *hacked off*)

slap and tickle: An alternative, if not entirely descriptive, phrase referring to the mating rituals of Homo Sapiens. 'A little slap and tickle never hurt anyone.' PETTING.

Slikka Pads: green plastic bladders filled with liquid (water?) which can be frozen and then put into a chilly bin to keep your picnic cold. (see: *chilly bin, coolibah*)

slip: This one shows. Slip is short for landslip, a minor landslide or SLIDE. This usually happens, as in the canyons of Los Angeles, when deforested areas get too much rain.

Smarties: One of the brand names for the candy known in North America as M&M's ('Melt in your mouth, not in your hand'.) (see: *Pebbles*)

smokes: CIGARETTES (see: *ciggies*)

smoko: COFFEE BREAK, also known as morning tea or afternoon tea, it all depends on how you like to spend your breaks.

snakes: There is no other evidence that Saint Patrick visited these shores but the total absence of snakes from New Zealand is certainly good circumstantial evidence. This absence has had some interesting results. A clinical psychologist friend calls 'Snake Phobia' the 'New Zealand phobia'. A Kiwi heading overseas for the first time is almost always worried about snakebite, to a certain extent, and otherwise sophisticated New Zealanders, when questioned about their expectations of other countries, surprisingly often come up with a fantasy about being met on the foreign tarmac by a carpet of slithering serpents.

snarf: to GOBBLE, as in eat. 'He snarfed up that steak as if he hadn't eaten for a week'. (see: *scoff, snavel*)

snavel: (A) TO GRAB. 'He snaveled every one of those biscuits off the tray before anyone else had a look in'.

    (B) to WOLF DOWN what you've grabbed. 'He snaveled his dinner like it was going out of style'. (see: *scoff, snarf, have a look in*)

snooker table: If you see something that looks like a pool table afflicted with elephantiasis, that's a snooker table.

Snowtex: The brand name for something that is exactly like KLEENEX right down to the box design. One thing, though, in New Zealand *Snowtex* has no competition. It has, like *Kleenex* in the United States, or *Biro* in New Zealand, become the word that describes the product as well as a brand name. (see: *Biro, Witches Britches*)

Social Credit Party: I don't understand Social Credit's policies. It's no excuse, but neither does anyone else of my acquaintance. Called the 'funny money' party by their opponents, popular wisdom has it that they would pay off the national debt just by printing more money. This has got to be too simplistic to be true. Social Credit is the third largest party in New Zealand and in the 1978 election got around 16% of the popular vote. Because of the geographic distribution of the vote, they only got one seat in Parliament. In my view, that was not unfair because it appeared that the majority of that 16% was registering a protest against their own party (National) rather than endorsing Social Credit. Their leader seems dynamic, intelligent and basically a nice guy. As for his major opponents (the National and Labour leaders), two out of three ain't bad. (see: *National Party, Labour Party, Values Party, Potty Party, Muldoon*)

**sod (you): Sod comes from sodomy and means to SODOMIZE. Not at all a genteel or friendly thing to say; it is an expression usually heard only in the heat of anger. A recent television comedy show used this as a gag line when an American lady turned up with her initials S.O.D. prominently displayed on her purse. (see: *homosexuality, bugger, false friends*)

solicitor: In England, attorneys at law come in two varieties. The backroom boys called solicitors, and the courtroom LAWYERS, called barristers. In New Zealand, as in the United States, these activities are usually combined in a single individual known as a 'Barrister and Solicitor'. (see: *false friends*)

solo parent: divorced, widow, widower, or unmarried mum, if you stay home to look after your kid(s) you are entitled to special payments from the Department of Social Welfare. However, this support can be lost if the Department has reason to believe that you are living with someone in a condition approximating marriage, and they are said to have evolved some elaborate measures which include the number of meals you take with a particular person of the opposite sex and the number of nights his or her car is parked in front of your residence. Social Welfare beneficiaries have been known to object to this surveillance and regulation of their sex lives. Furthermore, they maintain that, as enforced, the rules encourage promiscuity and discourage lasting relationships, as seven one night stands in a week wouldn't break the rules, but seven nights with the same person would.

something to go on with: SOMETHING FOR THE MEANTIME. It could be money. 'I'll pay you Friday but here is something to go on with till then'. It could be work. 'That big assignment won't be ready till tomorrow but here is something to go on with, read pages 21-50 in the Kiwi-Yankee Dictionary'.

South Auckland and **Bay of Plenty:** This is the center of the North Island including the Coromandel Peninsula to the north, Whakatane on the east and Lake Taupo in the south. The latter name was bestowed by a pleased Captain Cook who had just come from a much less hospitable area. The largest city is Hamilton whose metropolitan area comprises 94,777 people (1976). The whole area had 472,083 people (1976), 10,498,000 sheep and 2,684,437 cattle. Beautiful country, superb trout fishing around Taupo and thermal areas that make old faithful look as if it was misplaced. (see: *North Island*)

South Island: 58,192 square miles. The largest single chunk of land under the New Zealand flag. It has more sheep but fewer people than the North Island. The people (like me) who live there call it the mainland. There is a spectacular range of mountains, called with startling originality the Southern Alps, running down the spine of the South Island. This area provides good fishing, gorgeous hiking, skiing and for the adventurous exciting, if sometimes hairy, mountain climbing. (see: *Nelson, Marlborough, West Coast, Canterbury, Otago, Southland, mainland, North Island, Stewart Island*)

southerly: A wind from the south. Sound nice? This is a COLD WIND straight from the Antarctic wastes into your lap. In the southern hemisphere it is the word north that has echoes of sunshine, and summer, while the word south connates cold, snow, and winter. (see: *northerly, southern exposure, northern exposure, backwards*)

southern exposure: If your house has a southern exposure that means it faces toward the south. This is a no-no! South is from whence the COLD winds blow and where the sun never shines! Design your home with northern exposure and save on heating bills and cold discomfort. (see: *northern exposure, southerly, northerly, backwards*)

Southland: is defined in different ways for different purposes. Very roughly it consists of the south western part of the bottom of the South Island. Bounded on the east by the municipalities of Gore and Mataura, on the north by Queenstown and by Foveaux Strait to the south and the

Tasman Sea to the west. The best figures I can find give it a population of 108,860 people (1976), 331,000 cattle and 9,070,000 sheep. Rich grazing country, spectacularly beautiful in the west (see: *Fiordland*) and a bit chilly in the winter by New Zealand standards. The principal city is Invercargill (metropolitan area population 53,762 in 1976). (see: *South Island*)

Southland slippers: Much of (see:) *Southland* is farmland and when it rains venturing outside your farmhouse is a muddy business. So you keep a pair of RUBBER BOOTS on the porch and slip them on and off as you leave and enter the house. (see: *gumboots, Wellingtons*)

spanner: a WRENCH, you know, one of those devices for tightening bolts. (see: *long nosed pliers, bastard*)

(government) special work: If you are old enough to remember the 1930's CCC (Civilian Conservation Corps) camps, this should have a familiar if dismal ring. Any government agency, school, hospital board, university, voluntary agency etc. can ask the Labor Department to supply and fund someone who cannot otherwise get a job. These jobs last for a maximum of one year and are meant to provide work experience and training for those who might not otherwise get either. In addition, they are intended to enable jobs that are on the back shelf because of lack of labor to come to fruition. A similar scheme is operated for tertiary and secondary students during the summer. (see: *dole, seasons*)

speedo: the SPEEDOMETER in your car. If you hear a strange term used by a Kiwi, try to think of a longer word whose contraction it could be. What an incredibly awkward sentence! (see: *veges, beaut, strawbs*)

spencer: an item of LONG-SLEEVED LADIES UNDERWEAR, usually made of wool. Just the thing for those cold winter evenings indoors. (see: *singlet, central heating*)

*spew: THROW UP. An important term in the macho beer drinking society of young men. (see: *technicolour yawn, puke, chunder*)

spider: An ICE CREAM SODA, usually consisting of a dollop of vanilla ice cream in a *Coke*. (see: *false friends*)

split: 'What kind of split do you want with your drink?' What kind of MIXER would you like with your alcohol? (see: *spot*)

spot: a SHOT of booze. (see: *split*)

spot on: EXACTLY RIGHT, or hit the spot. 'Your dinner was spot on'. 'Her explanation of the economic situation was spot on'.

sprigs: The cross between spikes and cleats found on the bottoms of rugby boots (see: *rugby*)

sprog: (A) an INFANT.
 (B) any human OFFSPRING ('Your sprog')
 (C) 'I'm sprogged'. I'm PREGNANT. (see: *up the spout — up the duff*)

squiz: 'Have a squiz at that'. Have a LOOK at that. (see: *dekko*)

stand for office: It has been argued that the 'pace of life' is slower in New Zealand than in North America. Perhaps this is a reflection of that 'pace' since we must RUN where a (see:) Kiwi need merely stand.

standover merchant: Your friendly neighborhood PROTECTION RACKET OPERATOR.

starkers: what a streaker is: STARK NAKED.

s'story: THAT'S THE TRUTH or you're telling it like it is. 'Sam's a right bastard'. 's'story . (see: *quite*)

States or **Stateside:** Term used by American expatriates (temporary or permanent), voluntary or military to refer to the land of Uncle Sugar (Sam to you).

station: There are railway stations but the word usually refers to a farm or RANCH. (see: *cocky, high country station, false friends*)

steak and kidney pie: — speciality of the house. Served hot in a slightly leathery wheaten crust, this is one of the tastiest and cheapest snacks in New Zealand. About 40¢ (NZ) for a 3" diameter pie. Highly recommended. (see: *meat pie, hot pies, mince pies, savouries*)

Stewart Island: The smallest of New Zealand's three main islands (674 sq.miles), the least populous, 510 people, 219 beef cattle (1977), 40 cattle (1979) and the fastest breeding (and dying) sheep in New Zealand, a reported 3 in 1976, 5087 in 1977 and 3636 in 1979. It is almost THE MOST SOUTHERLY OF THE INHABITED islands. In fact, there is damn all, besides 3000 miles of water, between Stewart Island and Antarctica. Insofar as I can tell, Stewart Islanders, unlike their northern neighbors, have not entered the contest for the title of the mainland (see: *mainland, North Island, South Island*)

stipendiary magistrate: a JUDGE who gets paid; receives a stipend. The title of the judges who are on the first rung of New Zealand's three-tier justice system. The next two levels are the (see:) *Supreme Court,* and the Appeals Court.

stirrer: short for shitstirrer, a TROUBLEMAKER if you don't agree with them, a crusader if you do. If someone tells you that you've won the wooden spoon award, remember that it is given for excellence in the stirring sport.

stone: The weight of people (only) is calculated in stones. One stone equals 14 LBS. If someone says that he weighs 14 stone 9, he weighs 205 lbs. When it comes to human weights Kiwis think in stones and find the equivalent in lbs or kilos conceptually meaningless. (see: *pound, false friends*)

stones — stone fruit: stones are PITS and stone fruit are those cherries, apricots, plums, peaches etc. that have a pit.

stonkered: (A) WORN-OUT — exhausted. 'I'm stonkered. Wasn't in condition to do the Milford Track as a free walk, and I should have bloody well known it.' (see: *free walk, beggared, stuffed, buggered*)
    (B) INEBRIATED (see: *pissed, skinful*)

straight away: You can't race your car on this one. 'Do it straight away'. Do it IMMEDIATELY. (see: *false friends*)

strap: a verb suggesting energetic contact between a length of leather and a child's hand or rear end. (see: *get the strap, cane*)

strides: Not what you do but what you wear when you are doing it. TROUSERS. (see: *false friends*)

strong-eyed bitch, strong-eyed dog: WORKING DOGS (female and male respectively) that exercise remarkable control over flocks of sheep or herds of cattle or deer or horses or geese seemingly just by crouching down and staring at them. The dogs are in turn instructed by the farmer's whistles. (see: *huntaway, dog trials, dogs, cocky*)

stroppy: RECALCITRANT. 'Young Trev is getting stroppy. I told him to clean up his room and he told me to do it myself'. (see: *Bazzer*)

'struth: a contraction of 'God's truth', meaning, SO HELP ME GOD. 'I saw a U.F.O. last night 'struth.'

*stuff: ENGAGE IN SEXUAL INTERCOURSE; although I must admit this one sounds a bit one sided. (see: *shag, have it off, get one away, root, on with,* (a) *naughty, false friends, bit of crumpet*)

stuffed: (A) BEAT — worn out. It most probably originally referred to 'post coitum' (see: *stuff*). However, it is now a reasonably polite term for tired, no matter how this state was achieved. 'After playing footie, (football) all day, I was too stuffed to go to the party in the evening.' (see: *football, buggered, beggared, stonkered*)

(B) BROKEN. It was probably used at first to refer to worn out machinery, as it does to tired people, but has come to refer to any broken mechanism. 'This watch of mine is totally stuffed'.

sulky: No horses hitched to this one. Its a BABY BUGGY made OF woven CANE. (see: *pram, pushchair*)

sultana: An incompletely dried out RAISIN (usually from Australia). Sultanas, sometimes called golden raisins are juicier and tastier than raisins.

sun shower — summer shower: Remember California sunshine, the liquid kind that falls from the sky? This is a short RAINFALL WITH the SUN still SHINING brightly.

Sunday papers: The daily papers in New Zealand do not have Sunday editions. Instead there are a series of independent weekly papers dealing with sports and/or scandal. Most of these are nationwide papers (unlike the dailies) and could be fairly described as the YELLOW PRESS. (see: *Saturday paper, false friends, local rag*)

super: (A) superphosphate. The farmers' favorite FERTILIZER and one of the reasons for New Zealand's high pastoral productivity. It is usually spread by dropping it from light aircraft. Most of this super comes from aeons of layers of guano (bird droppings) deposited on the island of Nauru and which now gives Nauru the highest per capita income in the South Pacific. Unfortunately, this very natural resource is likely to be exhausted in around 20 years. The Nauru government and some consortiums of individuals are taking foresighted steps, investing their surplus capital in real estate and other income producing enterprises in New Zealand and Australia against the evil day when bedrock replaces birddrop. Nauru is also importing topsoil to put into the cleared areas which would otherwise be incapable of growing anything. (see: *aerial topdressing, manure*)

(B) superannuation. SOCIAL SECURITY or retirement income.

supper: A snack before retiring, never refers to the main evening meal. An evening party at home in New Zealand will almost always include a fairly substantial MEAL, called supper, SERVED 11:30-12:MIDNIGHT. (see: *dinner, tea*)

suspenders: aren't what holds up his pants, but rather what holds up her stockings. Suspenders are GARTERS and a suspender belt is a garter belt. (see: *braces, false friends*)

swedes: When the Vikings came to New Zealand Well, no! but it makes a good story. Swedes are RUTABAGA a very large variety with firm white flesh. Driving through the countryside at harvest time, you will see roadside signs saying swedes $2.50 (or whatever) a sack. (see: (to) *come off the turnips, marrow, beetroot*)

swept up: FANCY, elegant, elaborate. 'That's a swept up new car you've got'. (see: *flash, tarted up, false friends*)

switches: Light switches, appliance switches, all kinds of switches, they are all UPSIDE DOWN. Flipping up a switch turns it off; flipping it down turns it on. You may curse your own habits when trying to turn on a light in a dark room but take heart, there is a lot of U.S. gear, especially computer equipment, in New Zealand and the Kiwis find it just as hard to adapt as we do. (see: *hot points, backwards*)

swiz: a RIPOFF. 'It would take a major expedition to find any fruit in the fruit cake. What a swiz'.

swot: study-CRAM. 'I'm going to swot up on that subject'. During the period just before final exams, campuses are very thinly populated. Everyone is holed up, swotting.

swish: Ain't he sweet? How would you like to be called swish? Don't be upset. In New Zealand it is a compliment, meaning ELEGANT or SPIFFY. (see: *flash, false friends*)

T

T-bone: You know what a T-bone steak is, there's this big T shaped bone with a sirloin on one side and a fillet on the other. Well, in New Zealand, you get the bone and the sirloin but the fillet has been cut out for separate sale. (see: *fillet, butchery, false friends*)

ta: 'That was kind of you, ta.' That was kind of you, THANKS. (see: *thanks*)

ta-ta: BYE-BYE. To go to ta-tas is to go away. This is largely babytalk but as a cultural constant it is likely to be heard in almost any company.

T.A.B.: The Totalizator Agency Board; New Zealand's government owned BOOKIE PARLOR (betting shop for the Canucks). Takes bets as small as 50 cents on all of the trots and gallops in New Zealand and some of the Aussie ones. (see: *trots, gallops, punter, punting*)

tablespoon: equivalent to a large U.S. SERVING SPOON. (see: *false friends*)

take: Where you might hold out a tray of chocolate and say, 'HAVE one' a Kiwi would hold out the same tray and say 'take one'.

take a sickie: GOLDBRICKING. To take a day off ostensibly on account of sickness. 'Well, I was sick of work'. (see: *9 o'clock flu*)

take aways: food TO GO. Whenever I refer to food 'to go' my wife, who finds this phrase ridiculous for some unfathomable reason, says 'to go where?' Fast food places are called 'take away bars'.

(to) take the mickey out (of someone): is to RIDE them unmercifully. A friend recently described a scene in his local pub where someone was trying to take the mickey out of one of the local characters by imitating everything he did. After this had gone on for about thirty minutes the victim leapt upon the table and did a down trou. This was not imitated nor has any further attempt been made to take the mickey out of this particular character. (see: *down trou*)

take to scrapers: CHEESE IT. To depart at a RUN (take to your feet).

talk the hind leg off a horse: We all know somebody(s) with this unfortunate talent. A *longwinded* individual.

talking with a plum in his mouth: You are in no danger of facing this accusation. It suggests that the individual is AFFECTING AN UPPER CLASS ENGLISH ACCENT, putting on airs. (see: *pom — pommie*)

tallboy: This prospective basketball player is made of wood, stands about 5 ft. tall and has 4–5 drawers. It's the name for a TALL CHEST OF DRAWERS without a mirror mounted on top. (see: *lowboy, duchesse*)

tamarilloes: a goose egg sized and shaped red FRUIT with a hard outer rind (not eaten) and a jelly-like inside with scattered seeds looking like red passion-fruit pulp. The name tamarillo was especially invented for the United States market as the New Zealand name, (see:) *tree tomatoes*, was not considered either descriptive or glamorous enough. (see: *Chinese gooseberries*)

tandem: a BICYCLE BUILT FOR TWO. There are tandems for rent at most resorts, and even tandem races.

tangi: a tangi is a Maori funeral.

taniwha: pronounced tánifa. A SEA MONSTER in Maori legend. Of late he has been considered a benevolent monster. (Puff the magic dragon?)

tapu: TABOO e.g. burial grounds, tohunga, heads. Maori tapus still occasionally reroute roads or resite buildings. (see: *tohunga, tangi*)

Taranaki: Taranaki was named for its most prominent feature, (Taranaki is the Maori name for Mt. Egmont) a Fuji like perfect cone shaped volcanic mountain that stands 8,264 feet high in isolated splendor. It consists of a large peninsular bulge of land three-quarters of the way down the west coast of the North Island, known as a dairying area (see: *Taranaki gate*). The volcanic land is lush and productive. Population (1976 census) is 107,071 people; 1,907,000 sheep; and 703,000 cattle. The major metropolitan area surrounds and includes the city of New Plymouth having a population (1976) of 43,914. (see: *North Island*)

Taranaki Gate: An inexpensive and ingenious method of making a gate in your paddock fence. Named after one of New Zealand's richer dairying regions from which it has spread like gorse all over the countryside. This gate consists of two gateposts set deep in the earth. Firmly attached to one of the posts by loops of No. 8 fencing wire (the hinges) is a flexible, rectangular net of wire with a pole attached to the far end of the rectangle. This pole is in turn attached, top and bottom, to two loops of the same fencing wire that are firmly fastened to the farther gatepost. To open such a gate, you pull the top of the pole toward this gatepost and lift off the top loop. Then you let the pole sag in the other direction and lift it out of the bottom loop. To close the gate (and it is a gross misuse of hospitality not to), one reverses the process. The trick to closing the gate is to put the pole in that bottom loop first! (see: *cattle stop, Heath-Robinson apparatus, no. 8 fencing wire, gorse*)

tarted up: something basically not beautiful or fancy that has been GUSSIED UP. 'I tarted up my old bach by painting it yellow, then rented it to some American tourists for a month'. (see: *swept up, bach*)

Tatts: Tattersalls lottery, the Australian version of the Irish SWEEPSTAKES. In this case, it is based on the Melbourne Cup, the region's premier horserace. If you demonstrate that you are on a lucky streak, a friendly Kiwi might well tell you that you should 'rush out and buy a Tatts ticket.' (see: *Golden Kiwi, Bonus Bonds, gallops*)

tea: Refers to:

(1) Morning, pre breakfast cuppa

(2) Mid-morning 'coffee' break

(3) Mid-afternoon 'coffee' break

(4) Evening meal

(5) Occasionally any meal. As 'I'm going to get some tea'. 'Have you had your tea yet?'

(6) The familiar tannic drink. If you want it black, say so, otherwise it is served with milk. If you want it iced you won't be considered any stranger than someone who wanted boiled *Coke* would be in the States. If someone decides to indulge this peculiar request of yours, you are likely to get a small glass of tepid tea with a single, small ice block in it. Be properly grateful! (see: *dinner, supper, ice block, smoko*)

tea chest: The favorite box used for moving purposes is a foil lined PLYWOOD CRATE roughly two feet high, 16 inches wide and 20 inches long, (there are also square ones that would be 20 inches wide and long) which originally entered the country carrying tea from Sri Lanka (Ceylon), India or Bangladesh (West Pakistan). The tea was in loose flakes in the box, so that if you go to your local tea importer (at least one in every main center) and pay him around 50¢ you can purchase one of these excellent containers with a few tea leaves still kicking around in the bottom. The other source of Tea Chests is from people who have moved here from other tea drinking nations (Great Britain, Canada, South Africa), who have usually sent some or all of their belongings in this fashion. In fact, shipping companies in those countries and in New Zealand use the tea chest as a unit of measure. If you say, 'I want to ship a tea chest', they don't ask how big or how heavy (except by air) but merely tell you how much. A warning to any Kiwis planning to send one back from overseas. Shipment to New Zealand may be slow but not too expensive. However, unless you are prepared to arrange Forestry (it's made of wood) Dept., Agriculture Department and Customs clearance yourself, it will probably cost slightly more than it did to send it to New Zealand to get the local moving company consignee to do these things for you, effectively doubling the cost of shipment. You can, however, pay the consignee about ⅓ of this amount for the privilege of allowing you to do these things yourself. Set aside two to four hours. Things will go faster if you hit the Government Departments at 8.30 a.m. opening time, because they do not tend to be busy at this period.

tea towel: that old household standby, the DISHCLOTH. It gets a bit more use in New Zealand than in North America, since dishwashers are less common in Godzone. (see: *tea, Godzone*)

Teacher's College: If you are old enough to remember NORMAL SCHOOLS in the U.S. that's what this is. It takes New Zealand's equivalents of high school graduates and puts them through a three year course designed to train them as teachers. At the end of this period, the successful student will be awarded a 'Teaching Certificate', this is not the legal or moral equivalent of a B.A. or B.Sc. Teacher's Colleges are now starting to offer their brighter students the opportunity to gain a Bachelor's degree in conjunction with the Education Departments of nearby universities. University graduates who wish to go into teaching must spend a year at Teacher's College getting the practical training they've missed. They are then awarded a Teaching Certificate on top of their Bachelor's degree. (see: *Uni., varsity, college, Normal School, School Cert., U.E.*)

tear off a tab — **tear off a scab: is to OPEN a tear top CAN OF BEER. I must admit that the first time I heard the second description it made me too queasy to enjoy my beer. (see: *beer*)

technicolour yawn: To empty the contents of one's stomach through the oral orifice; often done as a response to an excess of alcohol in the system. (see: *spew, puke, chunder*)

telephone dials: As far as I can tell, New Zealand is the only place in the world where the numbers on telephone dials go from 9-0 rather than from 1-9 plus 0. Don't try to dial blind, you'll end up 180° out of phase. (see: *tolls, backwards*)

television licence: In the U.S. one must have a license to broadcast. In N.Z., as in Britain one must have a LICENSE TO OPERATE A TELEVISION RECEIVER. This license fee ($27.50 per annum for black and white and $45.00 per annum for color) helps support the two TV channels and provides one night a week (Sunday) blessedly without commercials. The payment of the license fee is enforced by a fleet of trucks (belonging to the (see:) *Post Office*) that can actually detect such operation. However, they are having one problem. Their equipment does not discriminate between color and black & white.

telly: Not Savalas although this is where you will see him; TELEVISION. (see: *goggle box, tranny*)

tena koe: pronounced tenáqway means ALOHA or hello and goodbye. You may hear this one on television when the weather is presented.

terms of trade: BALANCE OF PAYMENTS. New Zealand sells luxury goods overseas. You may not think of them as luxurious but most of the world does. Beef, lamb, wool etc. are what N.Z. lives on and most of the world can't afford, luxuries in these hard days. (see: *primary products, overseas funds, sheep*)

Territorials: The army RESERVES, weekend warriors, not to mention a fortnight in January. (see: *fortnight, January*)

test: a test match is a CHAMPIONSHIP game (of damn near anything, rugby most likely) between two teams representing different countries. One of these teams will be touring the other's country. Test matches have all the mystique of the world series, and Kiwis will stay up all night to see the satellite broadcast of such a game between New Zealand's touring All Black rugby team and that of Australia, England, Scotland or wherever the team happens to be. (see: *match, All Blacks, touring, side*)

thanks: I've noted elsewhere that one often says 'ta' rather than 'thanks'. Well, it is also common to say thanks rather than PLEASE. Rather like assuming your request will be complied with, and thanking in advance so you don't have to, afterward. 'Open the door, thanks'. Open the door, PLEASE. (see: *ta, the, false friends*)

that'll do me: THAT'S GOOD ENOUGH. 'How much do you want for that?' '$12.50.' 'Here is $11.00.' 'That'll do me.'

the: is often used instead of MY. 'The wife gave me a right bollicking when I came in late last night.' (see: *right, bollicking*)

theatre: in usual parlance, this refers only to the live theater, other terms being used for the movies. Almost every hamlet in New Zealand has its own amateur theater company, the main centers having five or six of these plus a professional or semi-professional company. (see: *main centre, dress circle, Opera House, Town Hall, Concert Chamber, flicks*)

'theft as a servant': Sounds much less grand (petty even) than EMBEZZLING. The old English value structure, if you work for somebody else, including large organizations, you are a servant. We retain the term for some purposes, e.g. public servant. (see: *Are you being served?*)

there's an old boot for every old sock: a phrase bearing reassurance for all those seeking spouse or paramour.

there must have been a stray bull in the paddock: A comment purporting to explain such genetic and reproductive anomalies as two blue eyed parents having a dark eyed child or the birth of a child to a woman whose husband has been in Antarctica for 11 months.

thousand million: 1,000,000,000 is equal to a U.S. BILLION. A U.S. billion is not equal to N.Z. billion by a factor of 100. (see: *billion, false friends*)

throw a wobbly: Young children are often specialists at this, but their adult counterparts are often capable of a spectacular TEMPER TANTRUM. (see: *do your bun, do a Hollywood*)

tickle the peter: To tickle the peter is to REMOVE MONEY FROM THE CASH REGISTER without recording the transaction. This could represent theft, or merely a reluctance to share with Inland Revenue. (see: *theft as a servant, Inland Revenue*)

tiddler: A tiddler is a LITTLE ONE. 'I saw the McKellar baby, she's just a tiddler.' 'I caught four fish yesterday, but they were all tiddlers so I threw them back.'

Tiki: Maori GOOD LUCK CHARM. I mentioned to a tourist guide in Auckland that I was a bit disturbed when the first thing his national airline did in Hawaii was hand me one of these good luck charms. He laughed and informed me that I had few worries on that score. The Tiki started out as a good luck charm all right — a fertility symbol worn only by women. (More recently, both pre- and post-European advent, men did take to wearing them.) Usually made of (see:) *greenstone.*

'time, gentlemen please': The signal that the PUB IS CLOSING, and you

103

must drink up and go. (see: *hotel, six o'clock swill*)

tin: There are no CANS in New Zealand, only 'tins'. Don't be deceived by the fact that the two objects appear identical. There is no such thing as a can; and so it follows that you put your garbage out for collection in the rubbish tin. (see: *rubbish*)

tip: (A) The tip is the GARBAGE DUMP. (see: *skip, rubbish, false friends*)

(B) Under most circumstances it is not customary to offer honoraria. Don't tip please! (see: *no tipping*)

to do (MATHS – ENGLISH – WELDING): Is to UNDERTAKE A COURSE OF STUDY in . . .

to get your face smacked in: BASHED. (see: *punch up, knuckle sandwich*)

toby: (A) the MASTER WATER VALVE for a building, ordinarily located under a metal cover in the sidewalk outside. Who was Toby anyway? 'Turn off the toby so I can fix the tap.'

(B) a brand of fishing lure.

toffee apple: Shades of carnivals and fairs, cotton candy and CANDY APPLES. (see: *candy floss*)

togs: Not all kinds of clothing, but only one kind. Bathing togs, or a BATHING SUIT.

toheroa: An ABALONE-LIKE SHELLFISH considered a great delicacy by most Kiwis. Open season on these is usually confined to five days per year on only two or three beaches across the country. Toheroa soup is canned and sold overseas, but the only place you can get it in New Zealand is in the larger tourist hotels. We found some cans in a Melbourne supermarket, and brought them back to New Zealand.

Tohunga: Maori WITCHDOCTOR, priest, wise man, scholar, etc. (see: *Maori*)

toilet: A toilet is a room by itself with only this facility in it. The room is customarily unheated, even in modern dwellings. This makes the 'toilet as library' habit an unusual one in New Zealand, particularly in the winter. (see: *loo, bathroom, toilet paper, lav, bog, grot, dunny*)

toilet paper: Unlike North America, where toilet paper all resembles facial tissue in texture, there are several grades in New Zealand. The most popular of these is about the texture of old newspaper. If you are settling in for a long stay or merely traveling around the country, you may wish to purchase some *Fluffy, Rx,* or (to my mind not quite as soft) *Swansdown.* On the other hand, if you come from corncob country the usual stuff (which I have carefully refrained from naming) may suit you just fine.

One more thing, the government purchases all their toilet paper in bulk and the wrappings on each and every sample reads: 'This Roll is the Property of the New Zealand Government.' I keep waiting to be asked to return after use. (see: *toilet, bathroom, grot, dunny, loo, lav, bog*)

tolls: Tolls is the branch of the Post Office cum telephone company that handles LONG DISTANCE telephone calls. When you dial for the long distance operator, she (or he) will answer 'tolls'. If you want to telephone overseas, dial 010 and ask for 'International'. Your local operator cannot directly put through an overseas call. (see: *call, telephone dials, Post Office*)

tomato/potato: Tomato is pronounced 'tow mat oh', potato is pronounced the way you learned it as a kid. Marvelous is the mind of man. (see: *tomato sauce*)

tomato sauce: If you were expecting ketchup, forget it. Ketchup can occasionally be purchased in small bottles sent out from England, but the standard tomato sauce in New Zealand is something else. It appears to be, in fact, just that. TOMATO SAUCE WITH NO PARTICULARLY NOTICE-ABLE added SPICES. (see: *tomato/potato*)

toning: MATCHING. As a toning skirt and blouse. (see: *twin-set and pearls*)

too right: 'That's too right mate.' That's a correct statement (opinion), and furthermore I AGREE WHOLEHEARTEDLY with my friend.

toot: One does not go on a toot in New Zealand. There are other ways to express this. One does, however, toot one's automobile horn as opposed to the rather vulgar American practice of HONKING it. (see: *on the piss, false friends*)

top dressing: The ACT of SPREADING FERTILIZER over a farmer's fields. This is often done from the air, and the fertilizer is most often super-phosphate. (see: *aerial top dressing, super, manure*)

top of the milk: As most Kiwis don't like their milk homogenized, a thick layer of CREAM accumulates at the top of your milk bottle. Many private recipes call not for cream, but top of the milk. (see: *milk, cream*)

topside: A rump roast of beef (see: *silverside, seasoned topside, butchery*)

torch: Put away your matches, a torch is a FLASHLIGHT. (see: *fire*)

touring: When a team of BALLPLAYERS (rugby, soccer, etc.) goes OVERSEAS to play against teams in other countries, they are touring and are often referred to as 'the tourists', as are foreign teams when they travel to New Zealand. (see: *All Blacks, test, side*)

town bike: This is teenage slang for the most ridden members of their female compatriots. Why aren't there any terms for promiscuous males? (see: *scrubber, lusty wench, Roman fingers*)

Town Hall: Not the seat of Government, but literally the TOWN MEETING HALL. Used for politics, entertainment, etc. it is most often the largest hall in town and is administered by the local government. (see: *dress circle, flicks, theatre, Opera House, Concert Chamber*)

trace wire: FISHING LEADER. (see: *bubble*)

trad: If it's trad, it's TRADITIONAL, and therefore sacrosanct.

traditional markets: For primary produce means GREAT BRITAIN. (see: *primary products, freezing workers*)

tramping: HIKING, what's that? In New Zealand one, strike that, everyone goes tramping. Ask your Kiwi acquaintances if they own tramping boots and sleeping-bags. The answer of, conservatively 98% will be 'of course'. (see: *free walk*)

tranny: That Japanese or Hong Kong made device on which we listen to the morning news. A TRANSISTOR RADIO. (see: *telly*)

trans-Tasman: The body of water separating New Zealand and Australia is called the Tasman Sea. Financially this is one of the widest bodies of water in the world, as it costs nearly as much to ship something across the Tasman as it does to ship it to or from the British Isles. Politically the gap is much smaller, but beware of thinking of Australia and New Zealand in one lump. In fact, at their nearest point, the two countries are 1,200 miles apart, have entirely separate governments and are always jockeying for position with each other. Like the Canadians say when talking about the U.S. 'going to bed with an elephant, even a friendly elephant, is risky business. He might roll over in the night and crush you.' Australia's 14,000,000 people looks elephantine compared to N.Z.'s 3,000,000. (see: A.N.Z.A.C., A.N.Z.U.S., N.A.F.T.A.)

tree tomatoes: You may know these as (see:) *tamarilloes*

trots: (A) MONTEZUMA'S REVENGE.

(B) That pursuit in which horses pull small carts containing single individuals around in circles in front of a large number of other people who have come to see them go round in circles and who place bets as to which horse, cart and driver will go round fastest. HARNESS RACING. (see: *gallops, T.A.B., punter, punting*)

trundler: A two-wheeled shopping basket used by those who would rather roll their purchases home than carry them there.

try: RUGBY TOUCHDOWN (3 pts). A conversion is worth 2. (see: *football, rugby, All Blacks*)

try it on: TO ATTEMPT SOMETHING, often used with regard to seduction or some new mode of employment for which you may not be qualified.

tuck in: 'Tuck into that kai, it'll line your stomach.' 'Eat that food . . .' (see: *tucker, kai*)

tupping: What the ram does with the ewe. (see: *service*)

turf out: THROW OUT.

21st: It is a New Zealand tradition that on a boy or girl's 21st BIRTHDAY, a large, coming of age PARTY is thrown. It used to be that this was the occasion for presenting, to the new adult, his or her first key to the parental house; symbolizing, and making possible the new freedom to come and go without supervision. 21sts still include the presentation of a key, but it tends to be three feet long, a foot wide, and made of foil covered cardboard these days. The symbol is all that is left as the real key (s? house, car, etc.) has most likely been in the pocket or purse, of the party so honored for some years.

twin set and pearls: Toning (matching) jumper (pullover, sweater) and cardigan (jacket style sweater) worn together and topped off by a string of pearls around the neck is winter uniform for the well dressed matron who is off to the bridge club or a job in which she meets the public. (see: *toning, jumper, cardigan, jersey*)

two toothed ewe: Most of the rams get slaughtered as lambs for export, as those N.Z. lamb chops your supermarket at home is hopefully trying to sell you. A few rams are kept for breeding and wool. Ewes, on the other hand, produce both lambs and wool so they are usually retained for these purposes. A two-toothed ewe is a TWO YEAR OLD FEMALE SHEEP. A prime age for breeding. (see: *hogget, sheep, primary products*)

U

U.E. or sit U.E.: This is the UNIVERSITY ENTRANCE certificate, which entitles those 6th formers (around 17 years old) to go to University. However, if they want to get financial support while attending, they must stay in High School another year and take additional exams. Some of those who earn this rating ($\simeq$82%) are accredited a U.E. pass without examination and some earn it through examination ($\simeq$18%). Of those who are candidates for the 'degree', either by accreditation or examination, approximately 42% fail and 58% pass each year. A more generous pass rate than School Certificate, but also a much more selected population, eliminating over 50% of the original population of pupils; those who did not sit School Certificate or failed it. (see: *school, School Cert, Bursary*)

U.K.: A common way of referring to the United Kingdom of England, Scotland, Ireland and Wales. i.e. The BRITISH ISLES. (see: *G.B.*)

Uni: UNIVERSITY. New Zealand has six of these: Auckland, Waikato (Hamilton), Massey (Palmerston North), Victoria (Wellington), Canterbury (Christchurch), and Otago (Dunedin); the last of these being the longest established. In addition there is Lincoln College, a tertiary level school of agriculture that grants a Bachelor's degree. The universities are divided into faculties (Arts, Science etc.) unlike U.S. institutions that are divided into colleges. (see: *varsity, Faculty, Teachers College, school, college*)

union bashing: The definition of this term (like others, see: *mainland*) depends on one's point of view:

(A) 'Unwarranted and heavy handed interference in the normal process of collective bargaining between employers and unions.'

(B) 'The ridiculously pejorative description of the Government's mild attempts to control the worst excesses of unnecessarily militant unions whose actions are imperilling the economy of the entire nation.'

In most cases, it would appear that justice resides somewhere between the two. (see: *F.O.L.*)

unit: (a) (Wellington only) suburban commuter train, car, SUPERFICIAL SUBWAY.

(b) A university course that runs all year and is the equivalent in time required of from 2-4 courses at a U.S. university. Only the University of Otago retains this system in New Zealand although in 1970 every New Zealand university operated this way. (see: *Uni, N.Z.R.*)

up himself: In practice this refers to someone who has a severely EXAGGERATED IDEA of HIS own IMPORTANCE) and/or qualifications, intelligence, etc. etc.). It derives from the suggestions that someone with such strong narcissistic tendencies could find only himself worthy of his own concupiscent attentions.

up to muster: If something is up to muster then it's all there or it's UP TO SCRATCH: This originates from comparing the number of soldiers who turned up when a company was assembled with the list muster roll of those who were supposed to be there. If they were all 'present and accounted for' the company was up to muster. See: *muster*

up the spout — up the duff: 'Milady, there's more in your belly than ever went in through your face,' (see: *bun in the oven, sprog*)

V

V8 gang: Teenage gang that specializes in using Yank tanks as transportation. An 8 cylinder engine being unusually large and powerful in N.Z. motoring. (see: *Yank tank*)

vacuum tube: The inner, glass part of your thermos flask that keeps your hot drinks hot and your cold ones cool. It has nothing to do with electronics pre-or post transistors. (see: *valve, false friends*)

Values Party: New Zealand's 'small is beautiful' people. 'Ride pushbikes instead of cars, exploit alternative sources of energy, reduce your material expectations and raise your spiritual ones, foreign capital is exploiting N.Z.' In 1975 they made a good bid to become N.Z.'s third major party. In 1978 they were almost ignored at the polling booths. However, this was partly because they had done a lot of 'consciousness raising' and as a result the major parties had adopted all of their more popular 1975 platform planks. The Values Party, despite its poor 1978 showing, still claims to be alive and well. Who knows? (see: *National Party, Labour Party, Social Credit Party, Potty Party*)

valve: (a) One of the vacuum tubes in your old radio or T.V. (see: *false friends*)

(b) A device for controlling the flow of (usually) liquids.

varsity: This is not a letter that you earn for athletic prowess, or the team representing your school, but another name for UNIVERSITY. The varsity is the university. 'Have you been to varsity?' is, Have you been to university? Only a limited proportion of the population goes to university, although anyone over 21 is welcome to try, and all those who have passed university entrance exams can enter at a younger age. It takes three years to earn an ordinary Bachelor's degree or four to earn a souped up Bachelor's called a Bachelor Honours degree. Despite the shorter period, I don't feel these students are any less qualified than their four year U.S. counterparts. (see: *Uni, Faculty, Teachers' College, college, honours, U.E., School Cert, false friends*)

Vegemite: (see: *Marmite* and *Vegemite*)

veges: VEGETABLES, another case where the Kiwi saves his breath. (see: *strawbs, speedo, beaut*)

vermin: You don't need a hunting license to hunt vermin Rats and mice? Well, yes, but also deer, wallabies, opossum, rabbits, etc. In other words, almost anything (other than birds) you might wish to hunt. The N.Z. opossum is not the same as the American one, it has a beautiful winter fur coat and these vermin skins go for $8-$15. Venison from wild shot animals can't be sold to the U.S. (regulations require inspection prior to slaughter) but can be sold to West Germany. The hunter can make over $500 for a big buck. (see: *false friends*)

vest: (A) An UNDERSHIRT, usually one made of cotton, worn by a man or a child. (see: *singlet, spencer, false friends*)

(B) (see: *WAISTCOAT*)

villa: Many of the Kiwis you meet will live in villas. Does this conjure up visions of vine laden elegance clinging to the cliffs above the French Riviera? Forget it! This is a one storied house, usually made of wood, otherwise known as a BUNGALOW. (see: *gentlemen's residence, property, false friends*)

Viyella: A wool cotton mix (55%–45%) favored for men's winter shirts.

W

wag school: 'It's a beautiful day, too nice to be inside. I'm going to wag school today.' It's . . . I'm going to PLAY HOOKEY today. (see: *9 o'clock flu*)

waistcoat: The third piece of a man's three piece suit; a VEST. (see: *vest*)

Waitangi Day: The Treaty of Waitangi ceding sovereignty over New Zealand to the British monarchy was signed on 6th February 1840. This Treaty has never been ratified by either the British or New Zealand Governments, and it never will be, because under its provisions the Maoris would own entirely too much of New Zealand. On the other hand, if it were ratified, the Maoris would be entitled to the rights and privileges of a freeborn Englishman of 1840. This would involve such considerable restrictions on their personal and economic liberty that I suspect, after a taste of the consequences, they would want to renege on the treaty. Modern Maoris would, of course, like to ratify the land provisions and ignore the others.

Despite the controversy and the fact that the Treaty will never be ratified, Waitangi Day is New Zealand's NATIONAL DAY as the 4th July is the U.S.'s (see: *Bastion Point*)

walking: One quickly adapts to driving ON THE LEFT hand side of the road, or the exercise becomes academic because you are dead and so is some luckless Kiwi. However, the 'rules of the road' also apply to walking, and you've been walking a lot longer than you've been driving. You walk on the right, use the right hand door etc. These habits have been reinforced and strengthened daily for every year of your life bar the first one or two. This means that you will find yourself performing an intricate dance when encountering a Kiwi on a narrow footpath, each of you reacting without conscious thought and neither understanding at first, why behavior that has been successful all your life isn't working. Imagine, you come face to face with a Kiwi on the footpath, you courteously and immediately take a step to your right, with equal unthinking courtesy, he takes a step to his left. You are still face to face. You take another unthinking step to your right, he takes another unthinking step to his left. You are still face to face. Ah! the light dawns, you take a step to your left, however, he has now figured out that if you are an idiot, you are at least a consistent one, so he takes a step to his right. You are still face to face, etc. etc. etc.

In small towns, this problem is less noticeable, but in Auckland, for example, there is a yellow line drawn down the middle of major sidewalks to remind you to keep to the left and you quickly wonder why all the world is going the wrong way. Similarly, when a building has only one door there is no problem, but when it has two you will head for the door to your right, while the Kiwi going the other way will head for the door to his left, and on and on it goes. (see: *driving, backwards*)

**wanker: There was a young lad who came across his parents engaged in exercising their marital prerogatives. He enquired as to the nature of this activity and was told that they were playing bridge. Later, his father found him in his bed and enquired as to the nature of his vigorous activity. The lad replied that he was playing bridge. His father then asked who was his partner in this enterprise. The lad said 'If you have a good hand, you don't need a partner'. This lad was a wanker.

This term is applied to any male you don't like, usually when he is out of earshot.

wardrobe: (A) a free-standing wooden CLOSET in which you hang your clothing. Older New Zealand homes assumed that you would have this piece of furniture and so these homes have no closets. For modern homes, the advertisements read 'built in wardrobes'. (see: *false friends*)

(B) Under specialized circumstances, wardrobe can refer to the clothing you put in the closet, e.g. 'The Wool Board has given Miss New Zealand a complete wardrobe entirely made of wool, so that she can represent New Zealand's products as well as its beauty at the Miss World competition . . .'

washhouse: A small outbuilding behind the main house where the LAUNDRY was traditionally done in a (see:) *copper*. These days, a modern or, not so modern (wringer washers are not uncommon) washer is likely to occupy this space. Dryers are considerably less common as sunlight and hot water cupboards seem to have some mystic virtue.

Modern homes usually have a washhouse built in. Rental properties, even unfurnished ones, almost always come equipped with a clothes-washing machine, of uncertain vintage, as well as a stove and fridge. It is a very unusual household indeed that sends clothing, bedclothes, etc. to the laundry. (see: *air the washing*)

watching the dicky bird: What you do when you are having your PICTURE TAKEN.

water: If you want some of this stuff in a restaurant, you must ask for it. When it comes it is likely to be served in a thimble, well a juice glass, and may perhaps contain a single ice cube as a sop to your accent.

If, however, you ask for a jug of water they will think you are nuts but will cheerfully provide one and wait to see if you were really serious about drinking it. (see: *ice blocks, beer, jug*)

water biscuit: A large, saltless CRACKER. (see: *biscuit*)

weather forecasts: I listened to these for years with mounting frustration since the official forecaster never utters a number, he only says: cold, cool, moderate, mild, warm and hot. An anguished appeal to the forecasters produced the following information (which I must admit hasn't helped much, you will see why):

cold (during winter 6° below normal)
cool
moderate (supposedly normal for place/time of year)

mild

warm

hot (during summer 15° above normal)

What may you ask is normal? That depends on where you are along N.Z.'s 1,000 mile north-south axis and when you are in the year. Assuming you have such a table handy (I suppose someone must have), then the above information should help.

wedding breakfast: The first meal after a wedding, whether at 6p.m. or 5a.m. The closest equivalent would be a WEDDING RECEPTION.

wee: New Zealand has a Scots heritage and a wee anything is a SMALL one. (see: *wees and poohs*)

week: A week in casual conversation tends to be EIGHT DAYS LONG. There is some confusion about the first day of the week, Monday being the most popular candidate, but Sunday having its adherents. (see: *fortnight*)

wees and poohs: This is young children's argot for URINATION and DEFECATION. My favorite story in this regard concerns the Kindergarten teacher who answered her telephone to find herself engaging in the following conversation with a caller who had a suspiciously high pitched voice:

caller: Is that Miss Kennecot?

Teacher: Yes

caller: This is an obscene phone call. WEES and POOHS! (see: *wee*)

Wellington: A very large region at the bottom of the North Island including the capital city of the same name whose metropolitan area has a (1976) population of 327,414 people. This region extends north as far as Lake Taupo, and in the north is bounded by Taranaki in the west and Hawkes Bay in the east. The region has 349,628 people most of whom live in and around the capital. There are also 11,787,000 non-voting sheep and 1,940,000 disenfranchised cattle in this region. The city of Wellington itself will remind you of a miniaturized San Francisco with Chicago's breezes. (see: *North Island*)

Wellingtons: This name has nothing to do with the city, despite what some spiteful Aucklanders might tell you. They are BOOTS. I'm sure the Duke's were leather, not rubber, but these are RAIN AND MUD PROTECTION, another name for (see: *gumboots, Southland slippers*)

West Coast — Westland: Kiwis think of this narrow strip of rain forest, backed up against the N.Z. Alps and their glaciers, as the frontier, the wild west. Lots of sandflies, very few people and a frontier atmosphere. Climb on a glacier, visit the Pancake Rocks at Punakaiki and take your insect repellent. The West Coast has 24,049 people, 196,000 sheep and 104,000 cattle. (see: *South Island, sandflies*)

wetback: An illegal Australian immigrant who has waded 1200 miles across the Tasman Sea. Well no, but it makes a good story. A wetback is a set of pipes or a *hot water drum attached to* the back or bottom of a *fire*place or solid fuel stove. This way you can have your fire, or cook your dinner, and heat your water at the same time with the waste heat, thereby saving electricity. (see: *trans-Tasman, wetback destructor, destructor, false friends*)

111

wetback destructor: A vicious method of ... A *small closed stove* for disposing of any burnable rubbish, this one is *equipped* with an attached *hot water drum* so that the waste heat is used to heat the water thereby killing two birds with one stone (see: *wetback, destructor, false friends*)

wharfies: Wharfies are STEVEDORES. They are members of one of the best paid unions in New Zealand because in a very real way, matched only by the freezing workers, they hold the nation's economy in their hands. New Zealand is a trading nation. That means that she sells her primary produce overseas and buys oil and manufactured articles. If she can't trade, everything grinds to a halt. In the 1950's the troops were called out to break a wharfies' strike. Things are quieter now, with most of the action coming from the freezing workers, but the docks remain one of the two most vital, vulnerable spots in the economy. (see: *seagulls, freezing workers, primary products, Terms of Trade, overseas funds, F.O.L.*)

what the guts is: *it all boils down to.* The two phrases seem to be related in sort of a cousinly way. Haggis anyone? (see: *guts*)

white goods: Kiwis rely on primary produce for most of their vital overseas trade. However, there are a few areas of manufacturing in which New Zealand excels. One of these is MAJOR HOUSEHOLD APPLIANCES (e.g. stoves, refrigerators, washing machines, etc.) or white goods. In fact, the Aussies are getting downright protectionistic about their inability to compete with these goods even with trans-Tasman (the Tasman Sea lies between New Zealand and Australia) freight rates (notoriously high) added. (see: *Aussie, NAFTA, trans-Tasman, primary products*)

white pointer: If you are out swimming and someone tells you that there is a white pointer about, don't look around for a bird dog. Instead, swim quietly (don't thrash about) to shore and then look out to sea for a WHITE POINTER SHARK. (see: *false friends*)

whitebait: A SMALL, literally TRANSPARENT FISH. The adult is called a smelt, but the past tense is misleading. The juvenile or Whitebait form is very tasty, baked into an omelet-based fritter called a 'whitebait fritter'. Whitebait are over fished and becoming scarce.

Whykickamoocow: An imaginary town located in the back of beyond; HICKSVILLE, NEW ZEALAND.

wicked: 'It's a bloody wicked day with a strong southerly blowing and the sky overcast.' It's a damn AWFUL day ... (see: *bloody, southerly, false friends*)

wigwam for a goose's bridle: an old unusual and uncommon Southland term for something that is *totally useless.* 'That's about as much use as a wigwam for a goose's bridle'.

Wilson's Whiskey and **'45 South:** NEW ZEALAND's OWN WHISKIES. Both are barley based, like scotch, but Wilson's is lighter and to my mind tastier than 45 South. I suspect bourbon drinkers would like these better than scotch drinkers.

windscreen: That part of the car that screens you from the wind; your WINDSHIELD. (see: *accelerator, boot, bonnet*)

windy: (see: *get the wind up*)

winge: Winge is a cross between whine and cringe. Some immigrants to

N.Z. are more vocal about their COMPLAINTS than others. One of these groups has become known as 'wingeing poms'. Unfortunately, when a group gets this label hung on them people cease to listen to the words. (see: *grizzle, bloody, pom*)

wink wink, nudge nudge: This has gone from being a series of meaningful gestures to becoming part of the spoken language with the same meaning. It indicates that you should read between the lines for unspoken innuendo, risque, or less than the letter of the law. 'That sheila is really built, wink wink, nudge nudge.' 'What the Inland Revenue don't know won't hurt them, wink wink, nudge nudge.' (see: *Inland Revenue, sheila*)

winter woollies: This term is used to apply to all thick winter wear. However, it most often refers to underwear (LONGJOHNS). (see: *central heating*)

wireless: That device developed by Marconi that carries voices between two points without intervening bits of copper. Despite T.V., RADIO is alive and well in N.Z. (see: *national programme, concert programme, B.C.N.Z.*)

Witches Britches: Believe it or not, this was a brand name for a fancy version of winter BLOOMERS for younger women. Like other brand names, this one has become a generic term (for ladies' long undies). (see: *knickers, Biro, Snowtex*)

within cooe: I think this one is on loan from the Aussies. Originally it meant within calling distance, but now it usually just means HANDY or around. 'Is your mate Bazzer within cooe?' Is your friend Barry around? (see: *Aussie, Bazzer, mate*)

(the) Wizard of Christchurch: An ex-sociology Lecturer from Australia has managed to convince the Christchurch City Council to appoint him town Wizard. He holds forth in the town square, wearing a loincloth (Alley Oop style) and occasionally whipping out a little white telephone on which he purports to talk to God. His off-duty costume includes top hat, tails and a silver headed cane (although he will on occasion wear this one with open sandals). He has founded a political party, the Imperial British Conservative Party, dedicated to re-establishing the Empire with (I suspect) Victoria as its head. Unfortunately, despite my approval of its other policies, I can't support this party because it is violently anti-Jewish and anti-Catholic which leaves a bad taste all round. The Wizard could safely be described as a hard shot. (see: *Lecturer, Potty Party, hard shot*)

***wog* or W.O.G.:** WORTHY ORIENTAL GENTLEMEN. When the British were in Egypt (the first time), the powers that were, felt that it would improve relationships with the local populace if their troops ceased to refer to their Egyptian counterparts as 'dirty black buggers' and similar endearing terms. Therefore, it was decreed that: 'Henceforth you will speak of the Egyptians as Worthy Oriental Gentlemen.' Wog is now an epithet applied to any non-European and just about as nasty as 'dirty black buggers'. We've a few of our own: wop, mick, kike, etc. (see: *boong, coconut*)

wonky: If something is a bit wonky its AWRY or ASKEW. 'There is something a bit wonky about that business deal.'

(a) **wooden aspro:** Prison argot for a clout on the head with a truncheon.

wops or wop-wops: Nothing at all to do with Italy. The wop-wops are the BOONDOCKS or BACKBLOCKS. (see: *booze, false friends*)

Words: Spelled differently but pronounced and meaning the same as their U.S. counterparts. The N.Z. (British) spellings below are, with three exceptions (rumour, savoury, marvellous) to be found as less preferred, but acceptable, variants in a standard U.S. dictionary. The British do not extend the same courtesy to the U.S. spellings. These lists are by no means exhaustive.

N.Z.	U.S. (preferred)
behaviour	behavior
centimetre	centimeter
centre	center
cheque	check
colour	color
favourite	favorite
flavour	flavor
gaol	jail
gramme	gram
harbour	harbor
honour	honor
kerb	curb
kilometre	kilometer
labour	labor
licence	license
litre	liter
marvellous	marvelous
neighbour	neighbor
practise	practice
parlour	parlor
programme	program
pyjamas	pajamas
rumour	rumor
savoury	savory
splendour	splendor
technicolour	technicolor
theatre	theater
travelled	traveled

(the) **works:** This is the meatworks or SLAUGHTERHOUSE for export lamb and beef. (see: *freezer, abattoir, freezing works*)

wouldn't have a clue: Somewhere between 'I don't know', and 'I don't bloody care'. (see: *bloody, oh yeah*)

wowser: A wowser started off to be a teetotaller, but has expanded in meaning to cover any sort of PURITAN attitudes.

X

X-rated: Only the journalist who is describing the book or movie has rated the entertainments so described. The government censors use a different system (see: *flicks*). This description is, however, widely used and understood to imply a high SALACIOUS content. (With thanks to Mrs Bear who provided a desperately needed X. Whoever heard of a dictionary that included only 25 letters?) (see: *Patricia Bartlett, flicks*)

Y

yachtie: A yachtie is a YACHTSMAN OR WOMAN. A representative of that substantial percentage of Kiwis who spend their free time sailing in one of New Zealand's many magnificent harbors or for those with larger craft, round the coast or even round the world. (see: *concrete yacht*)

yahoo: This one is courtesy of Jonathan Swift and *Gulliver's Travels*. Remember the brutish manlike creatures in the land of the intelligent horses? Well, a yahoo is a LOUT, and to 'yahoo around' is to do nothing constructive noisily. (see: *larrikin, yob-yobbo*)

Yank tank: This device does not bear General Sherman's name or that of any other general. It's your everyday V8 family CAR. In New Zealand, where the average car is *Toyota* sized and 4-cylinders, these rare dinosaurs look gigantic. Top this off with the 133% import duty and U.S. cars become fiscally impractical as well as oversize. (see: *V8 gang, mini*)

Yankee shout: GO DUTCH. (see: *shout*)

yob-yobbo: A yob is someone who is between slob and a lout. This term gets applied, almost exclusively, to young males. (see: *yahoo, larrikin*)

You shouldn't have done that!: A very sincere THANK YOU.

Your Worship: This is how MAYORS are formally addressed. In other circumstances, vilification is more probable than worship.

You're the dizzy limit: A description that hovers somewhere between exasperation and admiration.

Z

zed: The pronunciation of the 26th letter of the alphabet, the one we call ZEE. (see: *B.C.N.Z.*)

zippers: Another case in which the men's reflexes will betray them; you ladies are O.K. All jacket zippers for both sexes have the slide attached to the left hand side (as in ladies clothing in the U.S.). If you've been zipping up your jackets for years without looking at what you are doing, you are in for a culture shock. You can't do it, until you've totally retrained yourself. (see: *backwards*)